Japanese Hiragana for Beginners

First Steps to Mastering the Japanese Writing System

Timothy G Stout
Illustrated by Alexis Cowan

TUTTLE PUBLISHING
Toyko • Rutland, Vermont • Singapore

Published by Tuttle Publishing, an imprint of Periplus Editions (Hong Kong) Ltd., with editorial offices at 364 Innovation Drive, North Clarendon, Vermont 05759 U.S.A. and 130 Joo Seng Road #06-01, Singapore 368357.

ISBN-13: 978-4-8053-0877-6
ISBN-10: 4-8053-0877-X

Distributed by

North America, Latin America & Europe
Tuttle Publishing
364 Innovation Drive North Clarendon, VT 05759-9436 U.S.A.
Tel: 1 (802) 773-8930
Fax: 1 (802) 773-6993
info@tuttlepublishing.com
www.tuttlepublishing.com

Japan
Tuttle Publishing
Yaekari Building, 3rd Floor,
5-4-12 Osaki,
Shinagawa-ku,
Tokyo 141-0032
Tel: (81) 03 5437-0171
Fax: (81) 03 5437-0755
tuttle-sales@gol.com

Asia Pacific
Berkeley Books Pte. Ltd.
130 Joo Seng Road #06-01,
Singapore 368357
Tel: (65) 6280-1330
Fax: (65) 6280-6290
inquiries@periplus.com.sg
www.periplus.com

11 10 09 08 07   5 4 3 2 1

Printed in Singapore

TUTTLE PUBLISHING® is a registered trademark of Tuttle Publishing, a division of Periplus Editions (HK) Ltd.

Contents

Introduction

You probably picked up this book because you are interested in the best way to learn hiragana. If so, you came to the right place. The methods in this book have helped thousands of students in the United States and Japan to successfully learn hiragana, and they can help you too.

This book makes learning hiragana fast and effective by using clear explanations and examples and lots of fun exercises. It also features memorable picture mnemonics like the one below. Picture mnemonics enhance memory by associating the shape and sound of each hiragana character with pictures and English words already familiar to you. For example, the character "**mo**" as in "**mo**re" looks like a fishhook intersected by two lines, lending to the idea that "you can catch **mo**re fish with **mo**re bait."

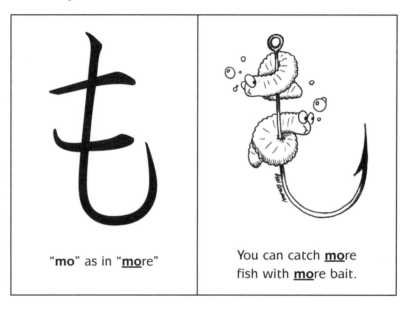

"**mo**" as in "**mo**re"	You can catch **mo**re fish with **mo**re bait.

How to Use This Book

An average, diligent student can learn to read the basic 46 hiragana characters in a few hours, and with persistence can learn to write them in a few short weeks. This introduction offers helpful tips on how to correctly pronounce and write the hiragana characters. It also discusses the origins of hiragana characters and the context in which they are used in modern Japanese.

The rest of the book is organized into three main sections. The first introduces the basic 46 hiragana characters along with writing tips and opportunities to practice writing them. The second teaches the usage rules that will allow you to write all of the sounds of Japanese and gives you more opportunities for practice. The third strengthens your skills through a wide range of exercises designed to both increase your knowledge of the Japanese language and reinforce your newly acquired writing skills.

At the end of the book you will fine a set of perforated cardstock flashcards and a list of suggested flashcard activities. Since it is easier to learn to recognize hiragana than to write it, you may want to begin with the flashcards, reviewing them often. As you learn to recognize the hiragana characters, you will find it much easier to write them. Whether you begin with the writing sections or the flashcards, you should plan on doing all of the activities for best results.

An Overview of the Japanese Writing System

Japanese uses four types of scripts: hiragana, katakana, kanji and romaji.

- **Hiragana** is a cursive set of 46 phonetic characters that express all of the sounds of Japanese. Hiragana is used mainly for writing the grammatical parts of sentences and native Japanese words for which there are no kanji.
- **Katakana** is an angular set of 46 phonetic characters, generally used for writing foreign words and for showing emphasis.
- **Kanji** are characters of ancient Chinese origin that represent ideas and sounds, and they are used for most nouns, verbs and other "content" words. There are 1,945 "common use" kanji that school children must learn by ninth grade. Romaji are roman (Latin) letters used to write Japanese; you must already know romaji since you are reading this.
- **Romaji** is used in textbooks and dictionaries for foreigners learning Japanese (and for Japanese people learning western languages) but their use in day-to-day writing is somewhat limited to things such as company names and acronyms.

ひらがな **Hiragana**	カタカナ **Katakana**	漢字 **Kanji**	**Romaji**

Don't be too intimidated by the number and seeming complexity of Japanese characters. Japan's 99 percent literacy rate[1] should allay any fears that learning Japanese is impossible. Compared to kanji, hiragana characters are not complex; each one only has between one and four strokes. Hiragana has only 46 characters, compared to the English alphabet which has 52 letters (26 upper case and 26 lower case). Although hiragana characters have a few more overall strokes than the letters of the alphabet, hiragana have a consistent one-to-one relationship between character and sound. By contrast more than half of the English alphabet letters have multiple pronunciations, and seemingly endless exceptions. Anyone who has learned the complexities of English spelling can succeed at learning hiragana. So, although learning hiragana may at first seem to be a Sumo-sized task, with the right training and practice you can do it! Before you know it you'll be a hiragana champion!

Hiragana is the first writing system that Japanese children learn. It is not uncommon for a four-year-old to be able to fluently read children's books and the like because of hiragana's simple one-to-one correspondence between characters and sounds. Hiragana can easily be used to write any word or phrase, and even adults will sometimes substitute hiragana for difficult or uncommon kanji characters.

[1] CIA World Fact Book Website 2002. Source: http://www.cia.gov/cia/publications/factbook/ viewed on May 10, 2006

According to the U.S. Foreign Service Institute, it takes approximately 1,300 hours[2] to acquire advanced Japanese proficiency, but much less time is required for basic proficiency. Hiragana is a great place to begin. The immediate benefits of learning hiragana include improving your pronunciation and gaining access to hundreds of dictionaries, textbooks, and other learning and enrichment materials written with hiragana. Plus, all of the writing skills of hiragana are transferable to learning katakana and kanji, making them easier to learn.

Don't rely on romaji. Foreigners learning Japanese sometimes rely on romaji, never learning to read and write. While it is possible to become quite proficient in speaking Japanese using only romaji, you will not be truly literate. Get comfortable using hiragana. When you buy a dictionary make sure it is written in hiragana, not romaji. When you write in Japanese use hiragana and katakana and kanji characters as you learn them.

Pronunciation Guide

Learning the pronunciation of hiragana is easy compared to English because there is a consistent one-to-one relationship between each character and sound (see a chart of The Basic 46 Hiragana Characters on page 10). The first five hiragana characters are the five vowels of Japanese. All example words use standard American English pronunciation. The English vowels tend to be slightly longer than their Japanese counterparts, which are pronounced as one syllable in length, short and clipped.

a as in f**a**ther and b**o**ther
i as in Hawa**ii** and b**ea**t
u as in gl**ue** and y**ou**th
e as in r**e**d and b**e**d
o as in **oa**k and b**o**ne

The remaining hiragana characters are consonant and vowel combinations, with the consonant always first (e.g., "**ka**," "**ki**," "**ku**," "**ke**" and "**ko**"). The one exception is the single consonant syllable "**n**" that is pronounced by touching the back of the tongue to the roof of the mouth, as in "i**nk**" and "si**ng**". Many Japanese consonants are commonly found in English, and are easy to pronounce.

k	as in **c**oat	**g**	as in **g**oat (voiced version of **k**)
s	as in **s**ue	**z**	as in **z**oo (voiced version of **s**)
t	as in **t**ie	**d**	as in **d**ye (voiced version of **t**)
n	as in **n**o		
h	as in **h**ouse		
p	as in **p**ig	**b**	as in **b**ig (voiced version of **p**)
m	as in **m**an		

Several Japanese consonants, however, are not commonly found in English and require special attention. One is the Japanese "**r**." In English, "**r**" is pronounced by curling the tongue so the sides touch the upper teeth, the tip of the tongue not touching. In Japanese, "**r**" is pronounced by tapping the tongue against the ridge behind the upper teeth, as in "pa**dd**le" and la**dd**er," sounding like a combination of "**l**" and "**d**"; it is not a rolling trill as in Spanish. "**tsu**" is pronounced as in "**tsu**nami" and "cat**'s** whiskers." "**fu**" is pronounced without touching the upper teeth and lower lip. It almost sounds like "**who**" and "**hoo**ting owl," except the lips are more pursed and air escapes more quickly.

There is a special consonant "**y**" as in "**y**arn," which is paired with the vowels "**a**," "**u**" and "**o**" to make the syllables "**ya**," "**yu**" and "**yo**." This consonant is special because Japanese use it extensively in combination with all of the other consonants to form additional syllables, such as "**kya**," "**kyu**" and "**kyo**" (see Section Two: Hiragana Usage Rules).

---

[2] Omaggio Hadley, Alice. 2001. *Teaching Language in Context*. Heinle and Heinle: Boston.

How to Write Hiragana

There are various styles used to write hiragana, but this book only uses the most standard **kyōkashotai** or "schoolbook" style. Hiragana characters are composed of three types of strokes: "stops," "jumps" and "brushes." With a stop, the pencil must come to a stop before it is removed from the paper. Jumps are written by removing the pencil from the paper as it moves to the next stroke. With a brush, the pencil is slowly removed from the paper as the stroke is written, giving it a tapered, sweeping appearance. In the example below, the character "**ke**" as in "**Ke**vin" is written with all three types of strokes. The first stroke is a jump, the second is a stop, and the third is a brush.

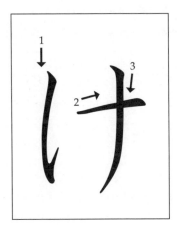

Writing the correct stroke types in the correct order is important for forming balanced, legible characters. With practice you will get the hang of it. You can make your characters look more authentic by slightly tilting left-to-right strokes, as in stroke two in "**ke**" (see above), rather than writing them straight across. Character strokes are generally written from left to right and top to bottom. Try to center each character in an imaginary box, not too far to the left, right, top or bottom.

Correct!	Wrong	Wrong	Wrong	Wrong
け	け	け	け	け

Traditionally Japanese was written from top to bottom, progressing in columns from right to left across the page. Now it is also commonly written from left to write, as with English. All the hiragana in this book is written from left to right.

Where Hiragana Came From

Although hiragana characters look like the picture mnemonics in this book, they did not originally come from pictures. Hiragana characters were developed based on simplified cursive-style kanji during the Heian Period (794-1185 AD)[3]. China, one of the great civilizations of the ancient world, had a huge influence on its Asian neighbors, including Japan. Kanji were first introduced to Japan around the 5th century AD.

The Japanese upper classes made a serious study of Chinese language, religion and government, and along with adopting new perspectives and practices, they adopted thousands of words and the kanji used to write them. The earliest official documents were written in Chinese, and for a long time Chinese was considered the language of the educated. Japanese also used kanji, however, to write poetry and prose in Japanese. This was

[3] National Museum of Japanese History Website. Source: http://www.rekihaku.ac.jp/english/ viewed on May 10, 2006

problematic since spoken Japanese and Chinese were very different, but the Japanese overcame this challenge by giving kanji new Japanese pronunciations, and by using some kanji as phonetic characters to be able to express native Japanese words and grammatical elements in writing.

Kanji used as phonetic characters were called kana or "borrowed names," implying that using kanji to express only sounds was not the regular practice. The first set of kana, called **man'yōgana** (the line above the "o" indicates it is two syllables in length), was difficult to read because there were no one-to-one relationships between the characters and sounds, plus there were hundreds of them. **Man'yōgana** was also difficult to write because each phonetic syllable had to be written in kanji. To simplify things, two sets of kana called katakana and hiragana were developed over time. Katakana or "partial kana" as the name suggests was developed from parts of kanji (see the following example).

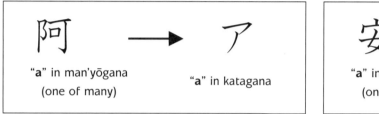

"**a**" in man'yōgana
(one of many)

"**a**" in katagana

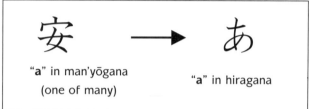

"**a**" in man'yōgana
(one of many)

"**a**" in hiragana

Writing with katakana was originally limited to men, and used in official documents. Hiragana or "common kana" was developed based on simplified versions of entire kanji characters (see example above). It was used in informal writing, such as letters and diaries, and it was referred to as **onna-de** or "woman's hand."

Ironically, during the Heian period while the men were attempting to write in "superior" Chinese, some women who learned to write in hiragana produced the finest literature of the period. *The Tale of Genji* written 1,000 years ago by a court lady named Murasaki Shikibu is generally regarded as the world's first novel, and a classic. In time, men began using hiragana as well. Today Japanese is written with a mix of hiragana, katakana, kanji and romaji.

The Tale of Genji by Murasaki Shikibu
is over 1000 pages in English translation.

Japanese Hiragana For Beginners is the right place to begin your Japanese studies. As you learn hiragana you will be taking the first steps to mastering the Japanese writing system and its pronunciation. Taking Japanese in small steps will make it more manageable. As the Japanese proverb states, "Even dust piled up becomes a mountain." or in other words, little things add up!

ちりも積もれば山となる

chiri mo tsumoreba yama to naru

(Even dust piled up becomes a mountain.)

Good luck as you embark on this new journey. As you increase your understanding of the Japanese people and their wonderful culture and language you will find fresh encouragement to carry on. One step at a time you can do anything. So, let's get started. Turn the page and begin your journey.

SECTION ONE

The Basic 46 Hiragana Characters

あ a	い i	う u	え e	お o
か ka	き ki	く ku	け ke	こ ko
さ sa	し shi	す su	せ se	そ so
た ta	ち chi	つ tsu	て te	と to
な na	に ni	ぬ nu	ね ne	の no
は ha (wa)*	ひ hi	ふ fu	へ he (e)*	ほ ho
ま ma	み mi	む mu	め me	も mo
や ya		ゆ yu		よ yo
ら ra	り ri	る ru	れ re	ろ ro
わ wa				を o**
ん n				

* These characters are pronounced differently when they are used as grammatical particles.

** This character is only used as a grammatical particle. It is not used to write words.

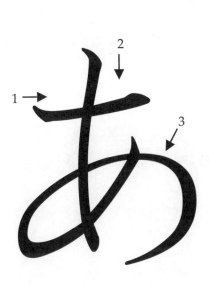

"**a**" as in f**a**ther

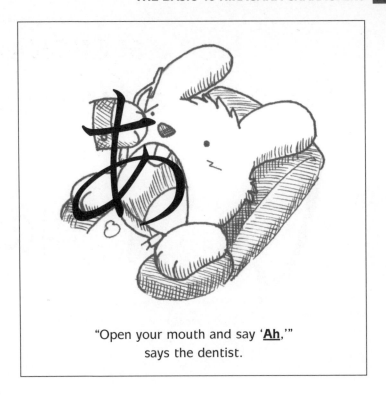

"Open your mouth and say '**Ah**,'" says the dentist.

Writing Tip "**a**" has three strokes: 1) a stop, 2) stop and 3) brush.

Trace these characters.

Write the character in the boxes below, and then circle the one you think is best.

1. **a ka** (red)

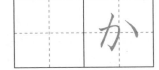

2. **a ri** (ant)

3. **a sa** (morning)

4. **a ki** (autumn)

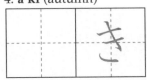

5. **a me** (rain; hard candy)

6. **a o** (blue)

"i" as in <u>ea</u>sy

the two "i"s in Hawa<u>ii</u>

Writing Tip "i" has two strokes: 1) a jump and 2) stop.

Trace these characters.

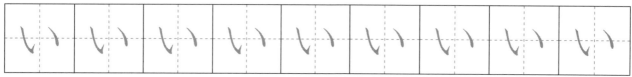

Write the character in the boxes below, and then circle the one you think is best.

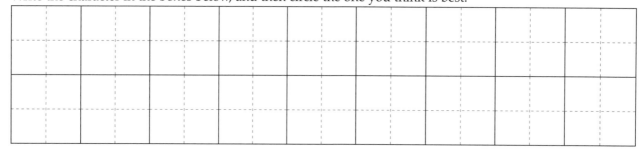

1. **i i** (good)

2. **i su** (chair)

3. **ha i** (Yes!)

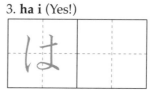

4. **o i shi i** (delicious)

5. **i ka** (squid)

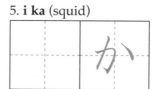

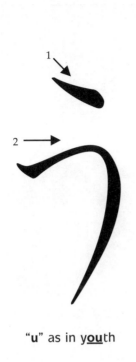

"**u**" as in y**ou**th

Ew! There's a bug on your ear!

Writing Tip "**u**" has two strokes: 1) a stop and 2) brush.

Trace these characters.

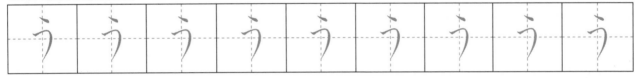

Write the character in the boxes below, and then circle the one you think is best.

1. **u chi** (home)

2. **u de** (arm)

3. **u e** (up)

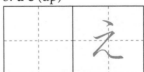

4. **u shi** (cow)

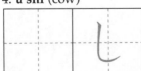

5. **u ma** (horse)

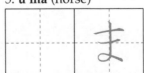

6. **u me** (plum)

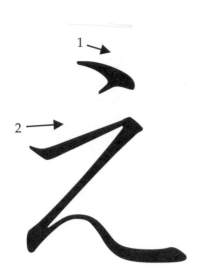

"**e**" as in r**e**d

An **e**lf is hanging ornaments
on a Christmas tree.

Writing Tip "**e**" has two strokes: 1) a jump and 2) zigzag stop.

Trace these characters.

Write the character in the boxes below, and then circle the one you think is best.

1. **eki** (train station)

2. **mae** (in front of)

3. **e e** (yes – colloquial)

4. **en** (yen)

5. **hae** (fly)

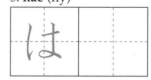

6. **ebi** (shrimp)

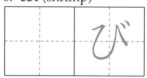

"o" as in <u>oa</u>k

<u>Oh</u>! A hole in one!

Writing Tip "o" has three strokes: 1) a stop, 2) brush and 3) stop.

Trace these characters.

Write the character in the boxes below, and then circle the one you think is best.

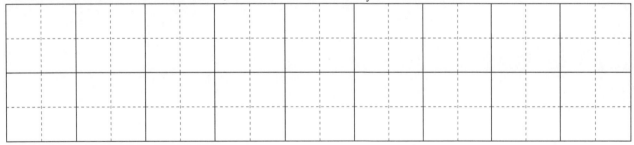

1. **ka o** (face)

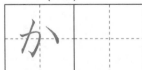

2. **o o ki i** (big)

3. **o ha shi** (chopsticks)

4. **o ka shi** (snacks)

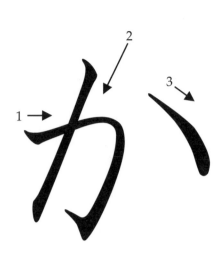

Kah! A crow cries as it flies to a tree on the top of a cliff.

"ka" as in **ca**r

Writing Tip "**ka**" has three strokes: 1) a jump, 2) stop and 3) stop.

Trace these characters.

Write the character in the boxes below, and then circle the one you think is best.

1. **mi ka n** (mandarin orange)

2. **ka** (mosquito)

3. **ka sa** (umbrella)

4. **chi ka** (basement)

5. **ka mi** (hair; paper; God)

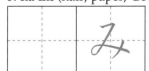

6. **na ka** (inside)

"ki" as in <u>key</u>

a <u>key</u>

Writing Tip "ki" has four strokes: 1) a stop, 2) stop, 3) jump and 4) stop.

Trace these characters.

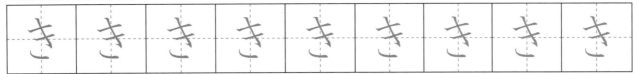

Write the character in the boxes below, and then circle the one you think is best.

1. yu ki (snow)

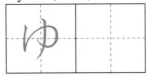

2. ki ta (north)

3. e ki (train station)

4. te n ki (weather)

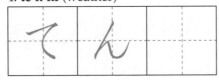

5. ki i ro (yellow)

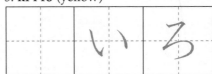

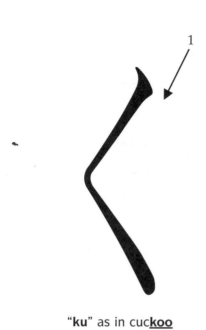

1

"**ku**" as in cuc**koo**

a cuc**koo**'s beak

Writing Tip "ku" has one stroke: a stop.

Trace these characters.

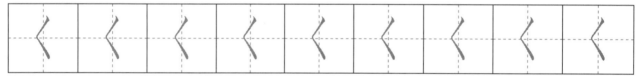

Write the character in the boxes below, and then circle the one you think is best.

1. **ku ro** (black)

2. **ku chi** (mouth)

3. **ni ku** (meat)

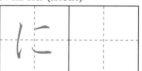

4. **ku tsu** (shoe)

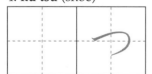

5. **ku ma** (bear)

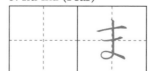

6. **ku mo** (spider; cloud)

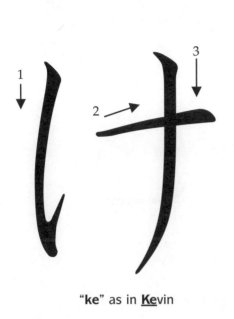

"**ke**" as in **Ke**vin

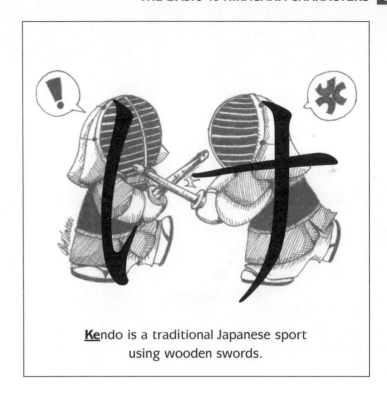

Kendo is a traditional Japanese sport using wooden swords.

Writing Tip "**ke**" has three strokes: 1) a jump, 2) stop and 3) brush.

Trace these characters.

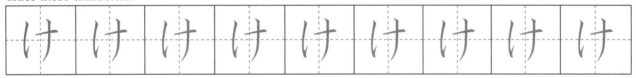

Write the character in the boxes below, and then circle the one you think is best.

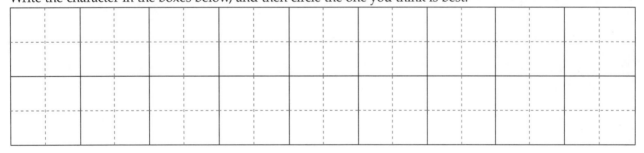

1. **ta ke** (bamboo)

2. **i ke** (pond)

3. **ke su** (to erase)

4. **to ke i** (clock)

5. **ta su ke te** (Help!)

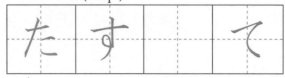

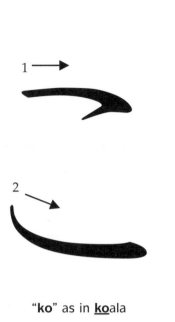

"**ko**" as in **ko**ala

A **ko**ala is climbing a tree.

Writing Tip "**ko**" has two strokes: 1) a jump and 2) stop.

Trace these characters.

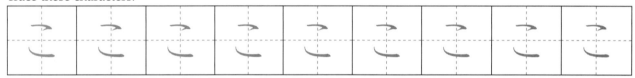

Write the character in the boxes below, and then circle the one you think is best.

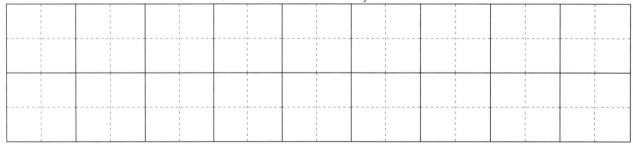

1. **ko re** (this)

2. **do ko** (where?)

3. **ko ko** (here)

4. **ko do mo** (child)

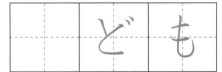

5. **i to ko** (cousin)

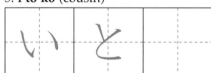

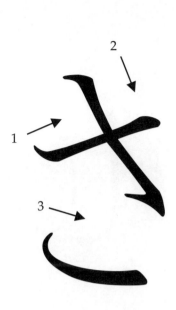

"sa" as in <u>sa</u>w

He <u>sa</u>w something that made him smile.

Writing Tip "sa" has three strokes: 1) a stop, 2) jump and 3) stop.

Trace these characters.

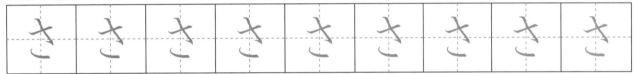

Write the character in the boxes below, and then circle the one you think is best.

1. **sa mu i** (cold)

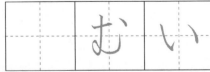

2. **ha sa mi** (scissors)

3. **sa n** (Mr / Mrs / Ms / Miss)

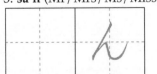

4. **sa n** (three)

5. **sa ru** (monkey)

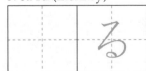

"shi" as in <u>she</u>

<u>She</u> has a ponytail.

Writing Tip "shi" has one stroke: a brush.

Trace these characters.

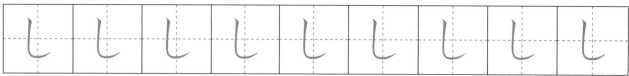

Write the character in the boxes below, and then circle the one you think is best.

1. **shi ro** (white)

2. **a shi** (legs)

3. **shi o** (salt)

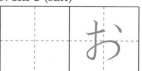

4. **mu shi** (insect)

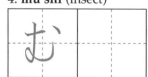

5. **shi ka** (deer)

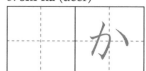

6. **na shi** (Asian pear)

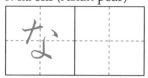

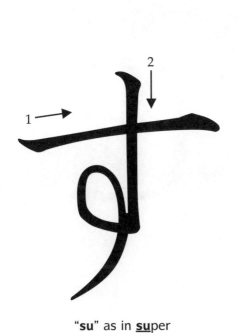

"su" as in <u>su</u>per

It's another perfect dive by <u>Su</u>per Diver.

Writing Tip "su" has two strokes: 1) a stop and 2) looping brush.

Trace these characters.

Write the character in the boxes below, and then circle the one you think is best.

1. **su** mō (sumo)

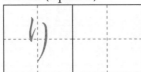

2. **su** (vinegar)

3. **su** shi (sushi)

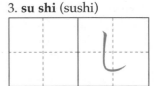

4. ri **su** (squirrel)

5. **su** ki (like – adjective)

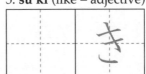

6. **su** ru (to do)

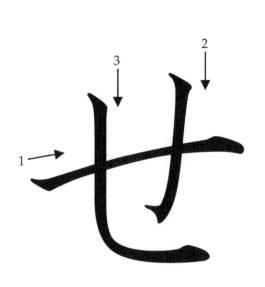

"**se**" as in **se**t

Mother **se**ts Baby on her lap.

Writing Tip "se" has three strokes: 1) a stop, 2) jump and 3) stop.

Trace these characters.

Write the character in the boxes below, and then circle the one you think is best.

1. **se n se i** (teacher; doctor; dentist)

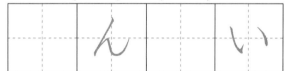

2. **se na ka** (a person's back)

3. **se mi** (cicada)

4. **se ki** (cough; seat)

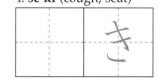

5. **se n** (one thousand)

"**so**" as in <u>sew</u>ing machine

Fix the rip by <u>sew</u>ing a zigzag stitch.

Writing Tip "so" has one stroke: a zigzag stop.

Trace these characters.

Write the character in the boxes below, and then circle the one you think is best.

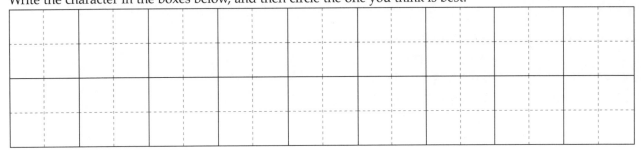

1. **so to** (outside)

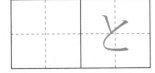

2. **so ko** (there)

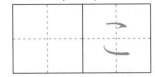

3. **so re** (that)

4. **so ba** (buckwheat noodles)

5. **so ra** (sky)

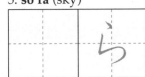

6. **u so** (lie; false)

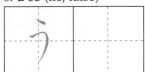

READING PRACTICE 1: あ 〜 そ

You should be able to read the words below now. Fold the page lengthwise (or cover it with your hand) so you can only see the hiragana words on the left hand side. Try reading them aloud and then check with the words on the right. Keep practicing until you can read them all. For an extra challenge try reading the Japanese and saying the English word before checking.

Hiragana	Romaji (English)
あ か	**a ka** (red)
あ お	**a o** (blue)
あ き	**a ki** (autumn)
い い	**i i** (good)
い す	**i su** (chair)
お い し い	**o i shi i** (delicious)
う え	**u e** (up, above)
う し	**u shi** (cow)
え き	**e ki** (train station)
え え	**e e** (yes – colloquial)
お お き い	**o o ki i** (big)
か	**ka** (mosquito)
か お	**ka o** (face)
お か し	**o ka shi** (snacks)
い け	**i ke** (pond)
け す	**ke su** (to erase)
こ こ	**ko ko** (here)
あ さ	**a sa** (morning)
か さ	**ka sa** (umbrella)
あ し	**a shi** (leg; foot)
し お	**shi o** (salt)
し か	**shi ka** (deer)
す	**su** (vinegar)
す し	**su shi** (sushi)
す き	**su ki** (like – adjective)
せ き	**se ki** (cough; seat)
そ こ	**so ko** (there)
う そ	**u so** (lie; false)

Romaji pronunciation guide:
a   as in **fa**ther and b**o**ther
i   as in Hawa**ii** and b**ea**t
u   as in **glu**e and y**ou**th
e   as in r**e**d and b**e**d
o   as in **oa**k and b**o**ne

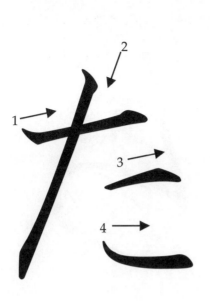

"**ta**" as in **ta**lk

"**t**" and "**a**" spell "**ta**"

Writing Tip "ta" has four strokes and all four are stops.

Trace these characters.

Write the character in the boxes below, and then circle the one you think is best.

1. **a ta ma** (head)

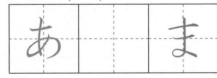

2. **ta no shi i** (fun; enjoyable)

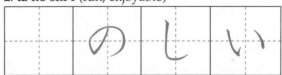

3. **i ta i** (Ouch!)

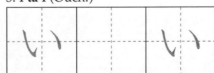

4. **ta ka i** (high; tall; expensive)

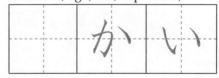

"**chi**" as in **chee**r

a **chee**rleader

Writing Tip "**chi**" has two strokes: 1) a stop and 2) brush.

Trace these characters.

Write the character in the boxes below, and then circle the one you think is best.

1. **i chi** (one)

2. **u chi** (home; house)

3. **ku chi** (mouth)

4. **mi chi** (road; path)

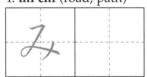

5. **shi chi** (seven)

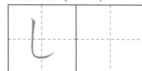

6. **ha chi** (eight; bee)

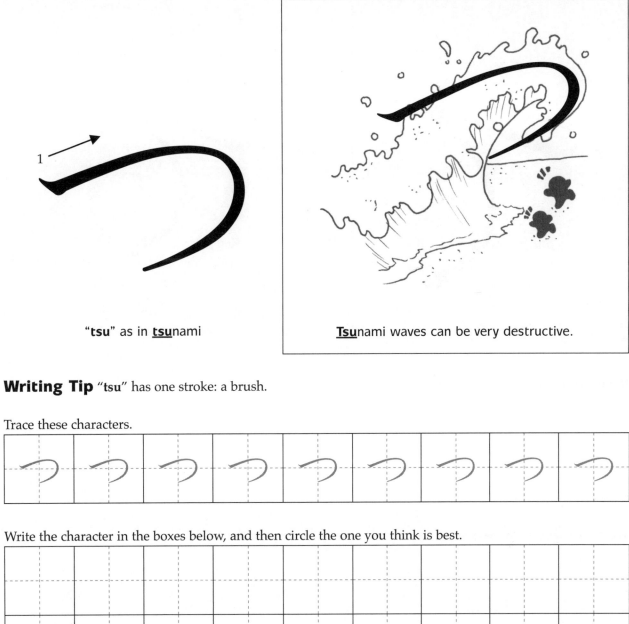

"**tsu**" as in <u>tsu</u>nami

<u>Tsu</u>nami waves can be very destructive.

Writing Tip "tsu" has one stroke: a brush.

Trace these characters.

Write the character in the boxes below, and then circle the one you think is best.

1. **a tsu i** (hot)

2. **tsu na mi** (tsunami wave)

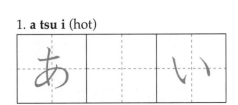

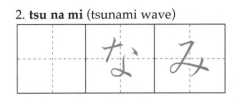

3. **i tsu** (when)

4. **ku tsu** (shoes)

5. **tsu yo i** (strong)

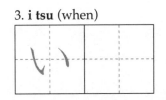

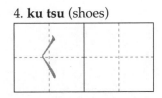

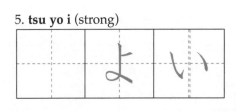

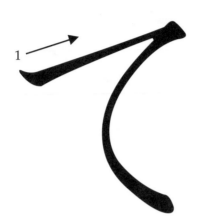

"**te**" as in <u>te</u>n

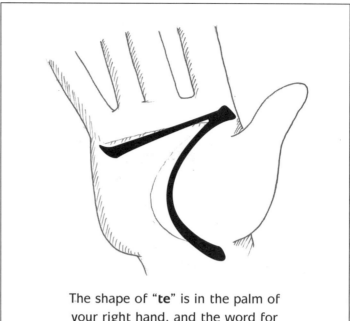

The shape of "**te**" is in the palm of your right hand, and the word for "hand" in Japanese is "**te**."

Writing Tip "te" has one stroke: a stop.

Trace these characters.

Write the character in the boxes below, and then circle the one you think is best.

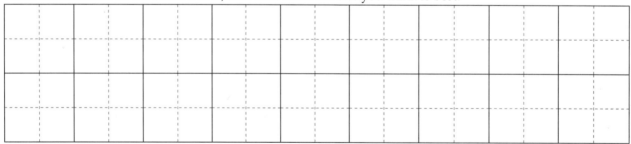

1. **te** (hand)

2. **ka ra te** (karate)

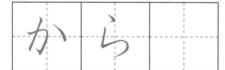

3. **su te ki** (lovely; cool; superb)

4. **chi ka te tsu** (subway)

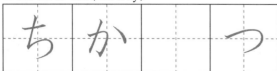

5. **te n ki** (weather)

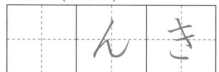

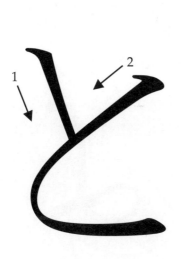

"**to**" as in <u>toe</u>

Ouch! There's a thorn in my <u>toe</u>!

Writing Tip "to" has two strokes and both are stops.

Trace these characters.

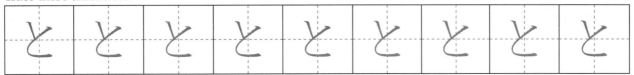

Write the character in the boxes below, and then circle the one you think is best.

1. **to** ra (tiger)

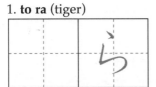

2. **to** ri (bird)

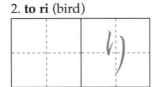

3. hi **to** (person)

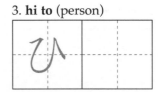

4. so **to** (outside)

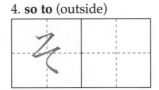

5. o **to to** i (day before yesterday)

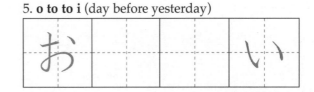

"na" as in to <u>gna</u>w

A beaver is <u>gna</u>wing on a tree.

Writing Tip "na" has four strokes: 1) a stop, 2) stop, 3) jump and 4) stop.

Trace these characters.

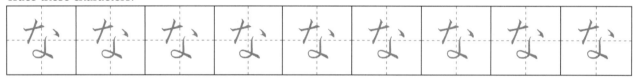

Write the character in the boxes below, and then circle the one you think is best.

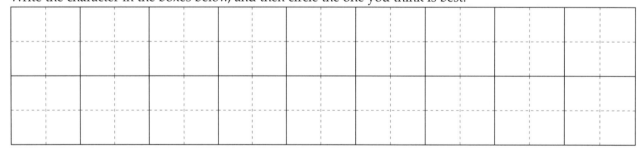

1. **na tsu** (summer)

2. **na ni** (what)

3. **na ka** (inside; middle)

4. **na me e** (name)

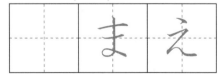

5. **mi n na** (all; everyone)

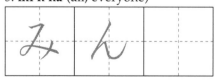

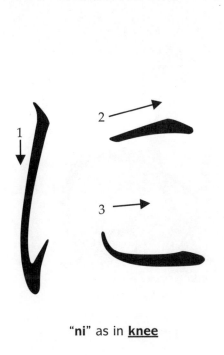

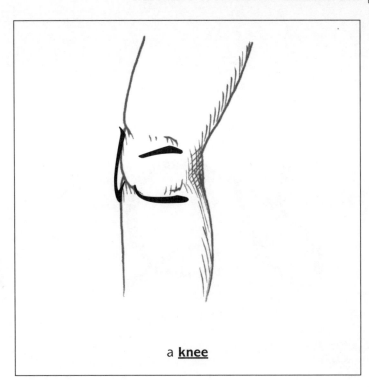

"ni" as in <u>knee</u>

a <u>knee</u>

Writing Tip "ni" has three strokes: 1) a jump, 2) stop and 3) stop.

Trace these characters.

Write the character in the boxes below, and then circle the one you think is best.

1. **ku ni** (country; nation)

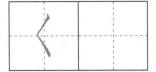

2. **ni ku** (meat)

3. **wa ni** (alligator)

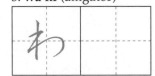

4. **ni ho n** (Japan)

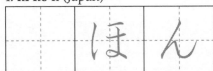

5. **ma i ni chi** (everyday)

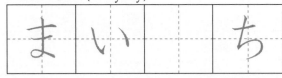

"nu" as in **ne**w

a **ne**w bicycle

Writing Tip "nu" has two strokes: 1) a stop and 2) looping stop.

Trace these characters.

Write the character in the boxes below, and then circle the one you think is best.

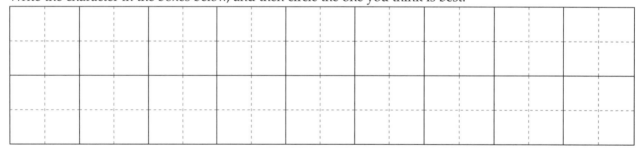

1. **i nu** (dog)

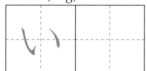

2. **nu i gu ru mi** (stuffed animal)

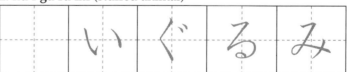

3. **shi nu** (to die)

4. **nu ru** (to paint; to color)

5. **nu ma** (swamp; pond)

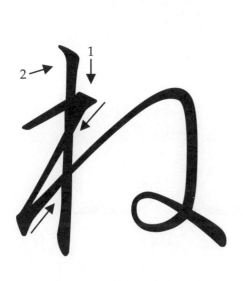

"**ne**" as in **ne**st

a **ne**st in a tree

Writing Tip "ne" has two strokes: 1) a stop and 2) zigzag, looping stop. (It looks like a "1," "7" and "2" all together).

Trace these characters.

Write the character in the boxes below, and then circle the one you think is best.

1. **ne ko** (cat)

2. **mu ne** (chest)

3. **o ka ne** (money)

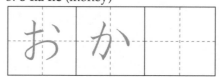

4. **ne ru** (to sleep; lie down)

5. **ne tsu** (fever; temperature)

6. **fu ne** (boat)

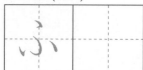

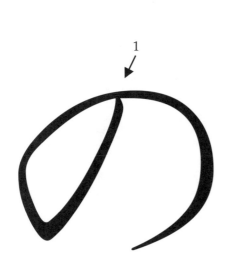

1

"**no**" as in <u>no</u>

<u>No</u> parking!

Writing Tip "**no**" has one stroke: a circling brush.

Trace these characters.

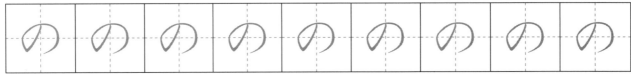

Write the character in the boxes below, and then circle the one you think is best.

1. **no ri** (glue)

2. **no do** (throat)

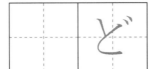

3. **mo no** (thing; object)

4. **no mi mono** (beverage; drink)

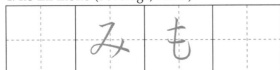

5. **ki nō** (yesterday)

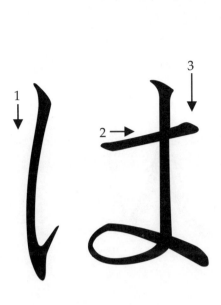

"**ha**" as in **ha**ll

a **ho**ckey player

Writing Tip "**ha**" has three strokes: 1) a jump, 2) stop and 3) looping stop.

Trace these characters.

Write the character in the boxes below, and then circle the one you think is best.

1. **ha ru** (spring)

2. **ha i** (Yes!)

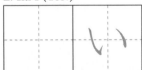

3. **ha ko** (box)

4. **ha sa mi** (scissors)

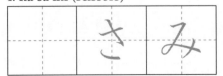

5. **ha** (tooth; teeth)

6. **ha re** (fine weather)

"**hi**" as in **he**.

He has a big smile on his face.

Writing Tip "hi" has one stroke: a sweeping stop.

Trace these characters.

Write the character in the boxes below, and then circle the one you think is best.

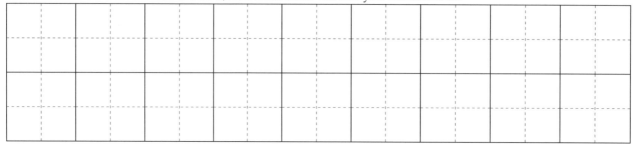

1. **hi to** (person)

2. **hi za** (knee; lap)

3. **hi ji** (elbow)

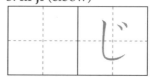

4. **hi** (fire; flame)

5. **hi ru** (noon; daytime)

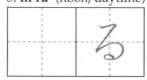

6. **hi tsu ji** (sheep)

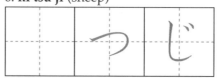

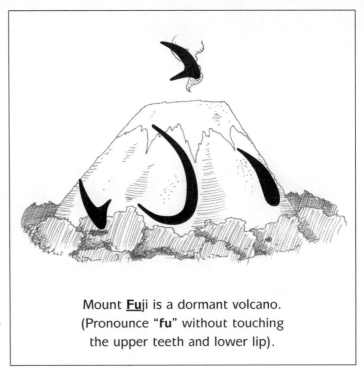

"**fu**" as in <u>who</u>
(except the lips are less rounded and more
air escapes from the mouth)

Mount <u>Fu</u>ji is a dormant volcano.
(Pronounce "**fu**" without touching
the upper teeth and lower lip).

Writing Tip "**fu**" has four strokes: 1) a jump, 2) brush, 3) jump and 4) stop.

Trace these characters.

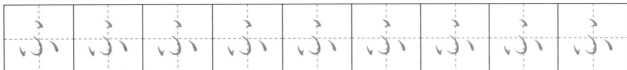

Write the character in the boxes below, and then circle the one you think is best.

1. **fu ji** (Mount Fuji)

2. **fu yu** (winter)

3. **tō fu** (tofu)

4. **fu to n** (futon mattress)

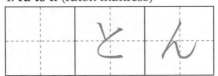

5. **o fu ro** (bathtub)

"**he**" as in **he**aven

an arrow pointing to **he**aven

Writing Tip "**he**" has one stroke: a stop.

Trace these characters.

Write the character in the boxes below, and then circle the one you think is best.

1. **he ya** (room; bedroom)

2. **he bi** (snake)

3. **he n** (odd; strange)

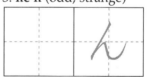

4. **he ta** (unskillful)

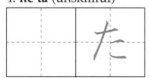

5. **o he so** (navel; belly button)

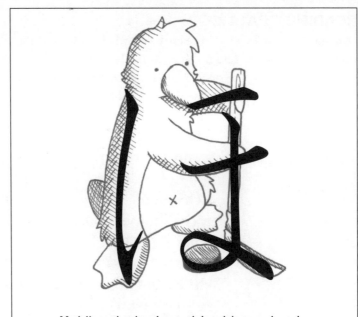

"**ho**" as in **ho**ld

Holding the hockey stick with two hands, he is ready to play!

Writing Tip "**ho**" has four strokes: 1) a jump, 2) stop, 3) stop and 4) looping stop.

Trace these characters.

Write the character in the boxes below, and then circle the one you think is best.

1. **ho** n (books)

2. **ho** shi (stars)

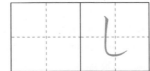

3. **ho** ne (bones)

4. e **ho** n (picture books)

5. **ho** so i (thin; slender)

READING PRACTICE 2: た ～ ほ

You should now be able to read the words below. Fold the page lengthwise (or cover it with your hand) so you can only see the hiragana words on the left hand side of the page. Try reading them aloud and then check with the words on the right. Keep practicing until you can read them all. For an extra challenge try reading the Japanese and saying the English word before checking.

い	た	い		**i ta i** (Ouch!)
た	の	し	い	**ta no shi i** (fun)
し	た			**shi ta** (under; below; tongue)
い	ち			**i chi** (one)
う	ち			**u chi** (home; house)
あ	つ	い		**a tsu i** (hot)
く	つ			**ku tsu** (shoes)
ち	か	て	つ	**chi ka te tsu** (subway; underground train)
ひ	と			**hi to** (person)
そ	と			**so to** (outside)
な	つ			**na tsu** (summer)
な	ま	え		**na ma e** (name)
く	に			**ku ni** (country; nation)
に	く			**ni ku** (meat)
い	ぬ			**i nu** (dog)
し	ぬ			**shi nu** (to die)
ね	こ			**ne ko** (cat)
お	か	ね		**o ka ne** (money)
も	の			**mo no** (thing; object)
は	い			**ha i** (Yes!)
は	こ			**ha ko** (box)
ひ	き	に	く	**hi ki ni ku** (ground meat; minced meat)
ひ				**hi** (fire; flame)
ふ	え			**fu e** (flute)
ふ	ゆ			**fu yu** (winter)
お	へ	そ		**o he so** (navel; belly button)
へ	た			**he ta** (unskillful)
ほ	そ	い		**ho so i** (thin; slender)
ほ	し			**ho shi** (stars)

Romaji pronunciation guide:

a	as in **father** and **bother**
i	as in **Hawaii** and **beat**
u	as in **glue** and **youth**
e	as in **red** and **bed**
o	as in **oak** and **bone**

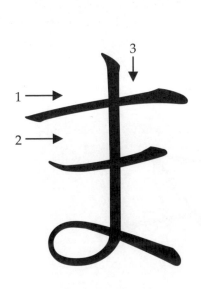

"ma" as in **mo**p

He will **mop** the floor.

Writing Tip "ma" has three strokes: 1) a stop, 2) stop and 3) a looping stop.

Trace these characters.

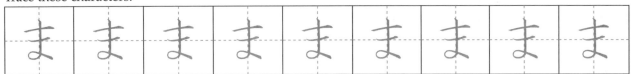

Write the character in the boxes below, and then circle the one you think is best.

1. **ma zu i** (unpleasant - taste or situation)

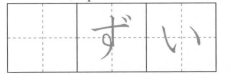

2. **a ma i** (sweet; indulgent)

3. **se ma i** (narrow; confining)

4. **i ma** (living room)

5. **ma do** (window)

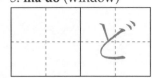

"mi" as in <u>me</u>

Who is number 21? <u>Me</u>!

Writing Tip "mi" has two strokes: 1) a looping stop and 2) brush.

Trace these characters.

Write the character in the boxes below, and then circle the one you think is best.

1. **mi mi** (ears)

2. **mi gi** (right hand side)

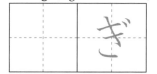

3. **mi zu** (water)

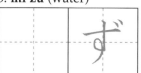

4. **ya su mi** (vacation; holiday)

5. **sa shi mi** (sliced raw fish)

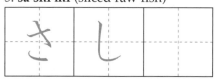

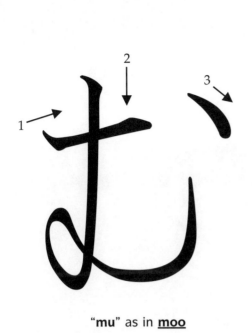

"mu" as in <u>moo</u>

<u>Moo</u>!

Writing Tip "mu" has three strokes: 1) a stop, 2) looping brush and 3) stop.

Trace these characters.

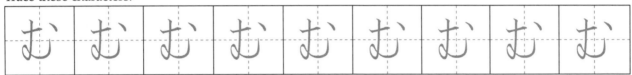

Write the character in the boxes below, and then circle the one you think is best.

1. **mu ra sa ki** (purple)

2. **sa mu ra i** (samurai warrior)

3. **ya su mu** (to rest; take a day off)

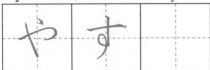

4. **no mu** (to drink)

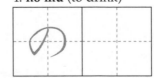

5. **su mu** (to live)

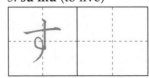

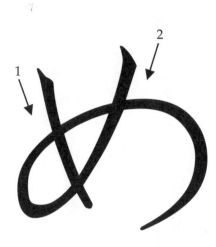

"**me**" as in **Me**xico

This bicycle needs a **me**chanic.

Writing Tip "**me**" has two strokes: 1) a stop and 2) looping brush.

Trace these characters.

Write the character in the boxes below, and then circle the one you think is best.

1. **me** (eyes)

2. **tsu me tai i** (cold to the touch)

3. **ka me** (turtle)

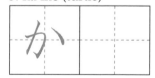

4. **tsu me** (fingernail)

5. **go me n na sa i** (I'm sorry.)

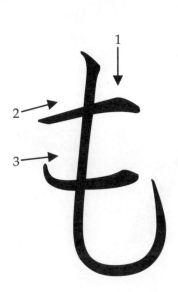

"**mo**" as in **mo**re

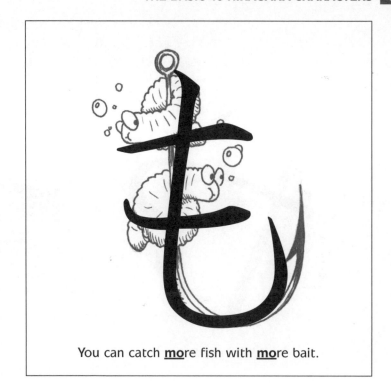

You can catch **mo**re fish with **mo**re bait.

Writing Tip "**mo**" has three strokes: 1) a brush, 2) stop and 3) stop.

Trace these characters.

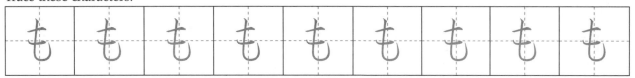

Write the character in the boxes below, and then circle the one you think is best.

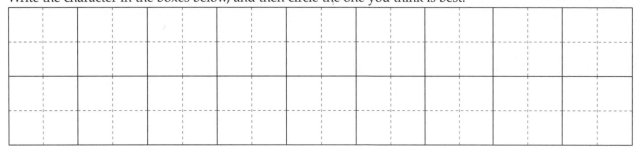

1. **mo mo** (peach)

2. **mo shi mo shi** (hello – on the phone)

3. **i tsu mo** (always)

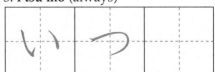

4. **to mo da chi** (friends)

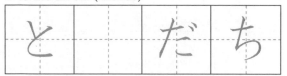

"**ya**" as in **ya**rn

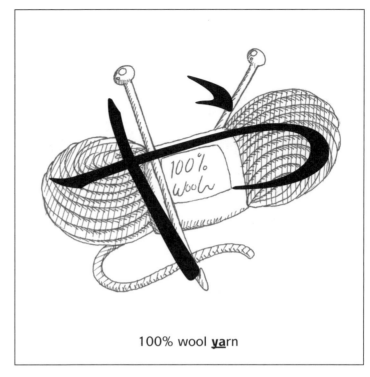

100% wool **ya**rn

Writing Tip "ya" has three strokes: 1) a brush, 2) jump and 3) stop.

Trace these characters.

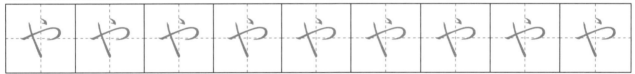

Write the character in the boxes below, and then circle the one you think is best.

1. **ya sa i** (vegetables)

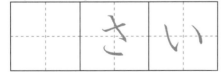

2. **ya su i** (inexpensive)

3. **ya o ya** (vegetable stand)

4. **ha ya i** (fast; early)

"**yu**" as in **you**

You stabbed the fish!

Writing Tip "yu" has two strokes and they are both brushes.

Trace these characters.

Write the character in the boxes below, and then circle the one you think is best.

1. **yu bi** (finger)

2. **yu ka** (floor)

3. **yu me** (dream)

4. **yū bi n** (mail; postal service)

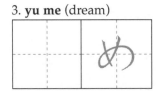

5. **yo yū** (spare – time, money, etc)

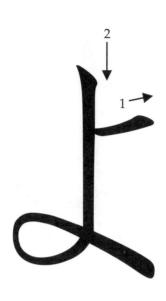
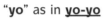

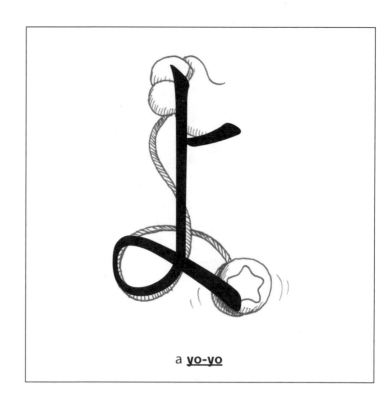

"yo" as in **yo-yo**

a **yo-yo**

Writing Tip "yo" has two strokes and both of them are stops.

Trace these characters.

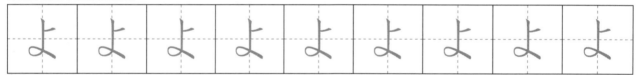

Write the character in the boxes below, and then circle the one you think is best.

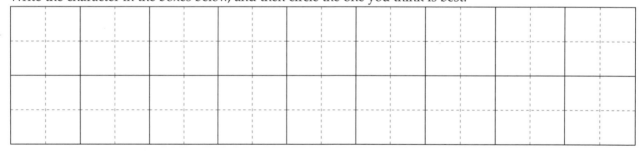

1. **yo ru** (evening; night)

2. **sa yo na ra** (goodbye)

3. **yo wa i** (weak)

4. **tsu yo i** (strong)

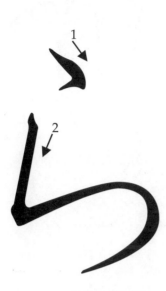

"ra" as in <u>Ra</u>h! <u>Ra</u>h! <u>Ra</u>h!

Using a megaphone the fan cheered for the team: <u>Ra</u>h! <u>Ra</u>h! <u>Ra</u>h!

Writing Tip "ra" has two strokes: 1) a jump and 2) brush.

Trace these characters.

Write the character in the boxes below, and then circle the one you think is best.

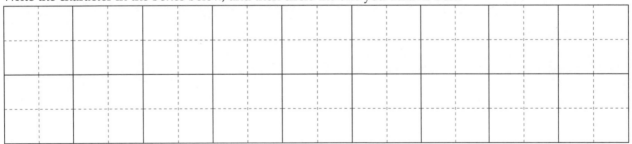

1. **o te a ra i** (restroom)

2. **i ku ra** (how much?)

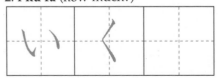

3. **ka ra i** (spicy; hot)

4. **ki ra i** (dislike – adjective)

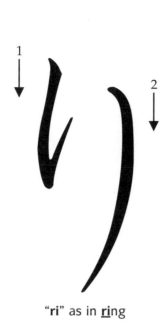

"ri" as in __ri__ng

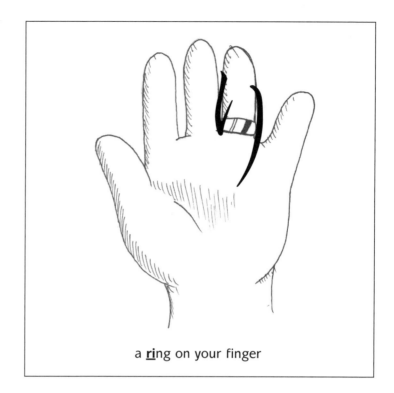

a __ri__ng on your finger

Writing Tip "ri" has two strokes: 1) a jump and 2) brush.

Trace these characters.

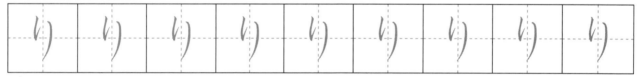

Write the character in the boxes below, and then circle the one you think is best.

1. **i ri gu chi** (entrance)

2. **ku su ri** (medicine)

3. **o tsu ri** (change - money)

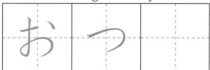

4. **ku mo ri** (cloudy)

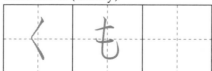

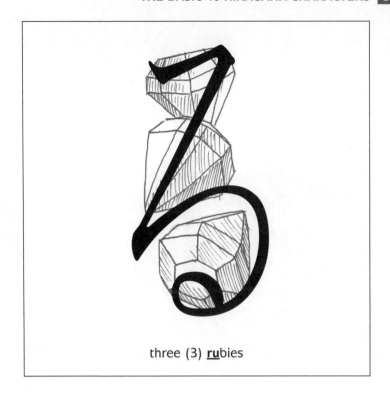

"**ru**" as in **ru**by

three (3) **ru**bies

Writing Tip "ru" has one stroke: a zigzag-looping stop.

Trace these characters.

Write the character in the boxes below, and then circle the one you think is best.

1. **fu ru i** (old - not person)

3. **ka e ru** (frog; to return home)

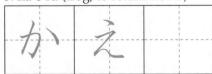

2. **a ru ku** (to walk)

4. **zu ru i** (unfair; cunning)

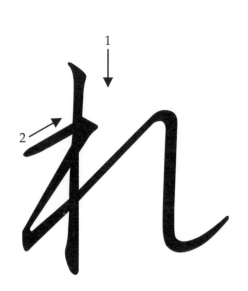

"**re**" as in **ra**dio

The **ra**dio tower was struck by lightning.

Writing Tip "**re**" has two strokes: 1) a stop and 2) zigzag brush.

Trace these characters.

Write the character in the boxes below, and then circle the one you think is best.

1. **da re** (who)

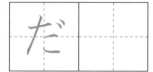

2. **ki re i** (pretty; clean; tidy)

3. **a re** (that over there)

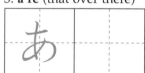

4. **u re shi i** (happy; glad)

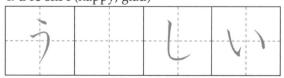

5. **i re ru** (to insert; to put in)

"ro" as in **ro**ll

The three (3) rubies **ro**lled away!

Writing Tip "**ro**" has one stroke: a zigzag brush.

Trace these characters.

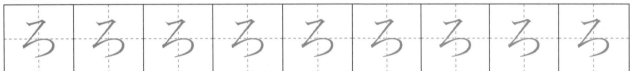

Write the character in the boxes below, and then circle the one you think is best.

1. **te bu ku ro** (gloves)

2. **u shi ro** (behind)

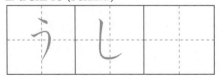

3. **hi ro i** (wide; spacious)

4. **da i do ko ro** (kitchen)

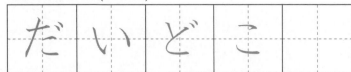

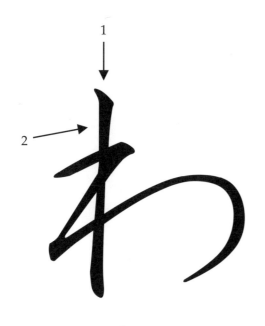
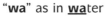

"**wa**" as in **wa**ter

A **wa**terfall is rushing past a tree.

Writing Tip "**wa**" has two strokes: 1) a stop and 2) zigzag brush.

Trace these characters.

Write the character in the boxes below, and then circle the one you think is best.

1. **wa ta shi** (I; myself)

2. **de n wa** (telephone)

3. **wa ru i** (bad)

4. **su wa ru** (to sit)

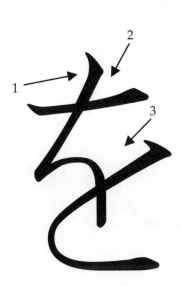

"**o**" as in **o**ld
(same pronunciation as お)

"Wh**oa**!" calls the cowboy to his horse.
(the "**w**" is dropped in modern Japanese)

Writing Tip "o" has three strokes and they are all stops.

Trace these characters.

を	を	を	を	を	を	を	を	を

Write the character in the boxes below, and then circle the one you think is best.

This character is not used to write words; it is a grammatical object marker (see Section Two).
Trace the light grey characters and write the character "o" by yourself.

1. **watashi wa sono hon o yomimasu** (I will read that book.)

わたし は そのほん ☐ よみます。

2. **dare ga momo o tabemashita ka** (Who ate the peach?)

だれ が もも ☐ たべましたか。

1

"**n**"as in **in**k
(pronounced by touching the back of the
tongue to the roof of the mouth)

The single consonant syllable "**n**" looks
and sounds a little like the English letter "**n**."

Writing Tip "n" has one stroke: a brush.

Trace these characters.

Write the character in the boxes below, and then circle the one you think is best.

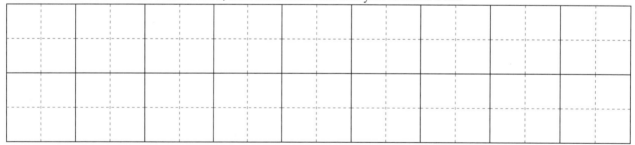

1. **su mi ma se n** (Excuse me.)

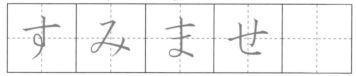

2. **e n** (Yen – money)

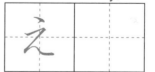

3. **ta n su** (chest of drawers)

4. **shi n shi tsu** (bedroom)

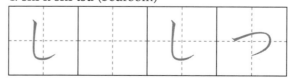

READING PRACTICE 3: ま～ん

You should now be able to read the words below. Fold the page lengthwise (or cover it with your hand) so you can only see the hiragana words on the left hand side of the page. Try reading them aloud and then check with the words on the right. Keep practicing until you can read them all. For an extra challenge try reading the Japanese and saying the English word before checking.

あ	ま	い		**a ma i** (sweet; indulgent)
い	ま			**i ma** (living room)
や	す	み		**ya su mi** (vacation; holiday)
み	み			**mi mi** (ears)
む	ら	さ	き	**mu ra sa ki** (purple)
さ	む	ら	い	**sa mu ra i** (samurai warrior)
め				**me** (eyes)
か	め			**ka me** (turtle)
も	し	も	し	**mo shi mo shi** (hello – on the phone)
も	も			**mo mo** (peach)
や	す	い		**ya su i** (inexpensive)
や	お	や		**ya o ya** (vegetable stand)
ゆ	か			**yu ka** (floor)
ゆ	め			**yu me** (dream)
さ	よ	な	ら	**sa yo na ra** (goodbye)
よ	る			**yo ru** (evening; night)
い	く	ら		**i ku ra** (how much)
か	ら	い		**ka ra i** (spicy; hot)
お	つ	り		**o tsu ri** (change – money)
く	す	り		**ku su ri** (medicine)
ふ	る	い		**fu ru i** (old – not person)
か	え	る		**ka e ru** (frog; to return home)
き	れ	い		**ki re i** (pretty; clean; tidy)
う	れ	し	い	**u re shi i** (happy; glad)
ひ	ろ	い		**hi ro i** (wide; spacious)
う	し	ろ		**u shi ro** (behind)
わ	た	し		**wa ta shi** (I; myself)
か	わ	い	い	**ka wa i i** (cute)
え	ん			**e n** (yen – Japanese money)

Romaji pronunciation guide:

a   as in **f**a**ther and **b**o**ther

i   as in Ha**w**ai**i and **b**ea**t

u   as in gl**u**e and y**ou**th

e   as in r**e**d and **b**e**d

o   as in **o**ak and b**o**ne

SECTION TWO
Hiragana Usage Rules

THE ADDITIONAL 58 HIRAGANA SOUNDS

が ga	ぎ gi	ぐ gu	げ ge	ご go
ざ za	じ ji	ず zu	ぜ ze	ぞ zo
だ da	ぢ ji*	づ zu*	で de	ど do
ば ba	び bi	ぶ bu	べ be	ぼ bo
ぱ pa	ぴ pi	ぷ pu	ぺ pe	ぽ po

* "**ji**" and "**zu**" are usually written with じ and ず.

きゃ kya	きゅ kyu	きょ kyo
しゃ sha	しゅ shu	しょ sho
ちゃ cha	ちゅ chu	ちょ cho
にゃ nya	にゅ nyu	にょ nyo
ひゃ hya	ひゅ hyu	ひょ hyo

みゃ mya	みゅ myu	みょ myo
りゃ rya	りゅ ryu	りょ ryo

ぎゃ gya	ぎゅ gyu	ぎょ gyo
じゃ ja	じゅ ju	じょ jo
ぢゃ ja*	ぢゅ ju*	ぢょ jo*

* "**ja**," "**ju**" and "**jo**" are usually written with じゃ, じゅ and じょ.

びゃ bya	びゅ byu	びょ byo
ぴゃ pya	ぴゅ pyu	ぴょ pyo

Japanese learners are lucky that there are so few hiragana rules. Mastering all the rules (and exceptions) in English takes years of spelling tests. In Japanese, however, once you have learned the five basic rules of hiragana you will be able to write 58 sounds using the 46 hiragana characters already introduced, and write any word you like.

RULE 1   TENTEN (˝) AND MARU (°)

The first rule describes the way the pronunciation changes when two small dashes (˝) called **tenten** or a small circle (°) called **maru** is added to a hiragana character. Tenten may be added to 20 hiragana characters, giving them a voiced consonant sound. For example, adding tenten to any of the か, き, く, け, こ row characters changes the "**k**" (as in **coat**) to "**g**" (as in **goat**). You will notice a vibration in your throat when you pronounce "**g**," but not "**k**." All 20 hiragana characters become voiced sounds when you add tenten.

k˝ → g as in "goat"   t˝ → d as in "dye"   Except じ = **ji** (as in "jeans")
s˝ → z as in "zoo"   h˝ → b as in "big"   ぢ = **ji** (as in "jeans")
　　　　　　　　　　　　　　　　　　　　　　　　づ = **zu** (as in "zoo")

You may have noticed that there are two ways to write the sounds "**ji**" and "**zu**." In most cases "**ji**" and "**zu**" are written じ and ず.

Maru (°) are only added to the hiragana characters は, ひ, ふ, へ, ほ. They become ぱ, ぴ, ぷ, ぺ, ぽ and they are pronounced "**pa**," "**pi**," "**pu**," "**pe**," "**po**."

h° → p as in "pig"

Writing Practice: Say the sounds aloud as you write these hiragana characters with tenten and maru. Trace the light grey characters and then complete the row by yourself.

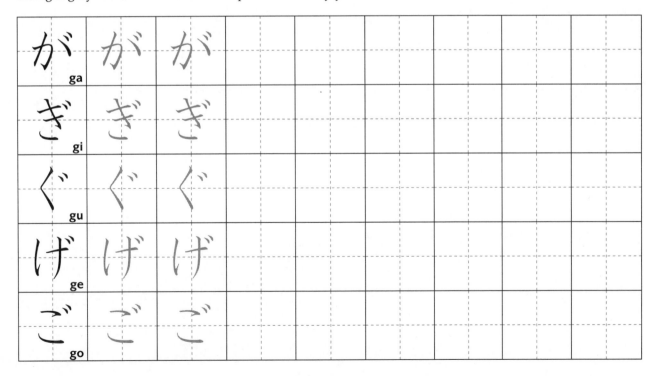

Now try writing the following words that use the first group of characters written with tenten. Trace the light grey characters, and then write the appropriate character in the blank box.

1. **hi ra ga na** (hiragana)

2. **ma n ga** (comics)

3. **o ni gi ri** (rice ball)

4. **mi gi** (right hand side)

5. **i ri gu chi** (entrance)

6. **o yo gu** (to swim)

7. **ge n ka n** (entryway of a Japanese home)

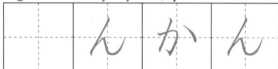

8. **ge n ki** (fine, healthy)

9. **ni ho n go** (Japanese language)

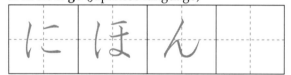

10. **go ha n** (rice; food)

11. **me ga ne** (glasses)

12. **u sa gi** (rabbit)

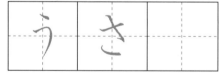

13. **hi ge** (mustache, beard)

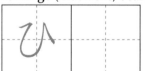

14. **de gu chi** (exit)

The second group of characters written with tenten has one exception: じ is pronounced "**ji**."

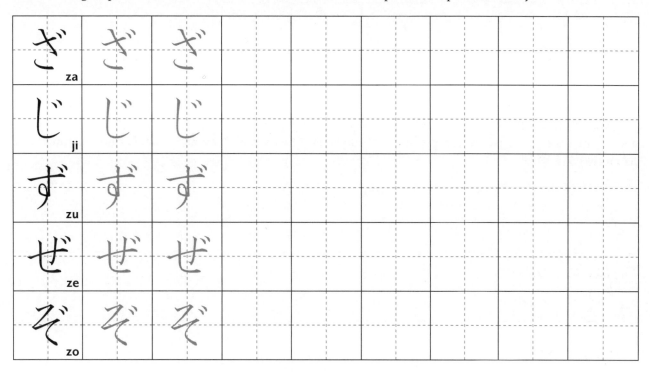

Try writing these words that use the second group of tenten characters.

1. za n ne n (unfortunate; too bad)

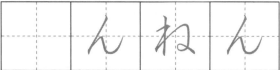

2. hi za (knee; lap)

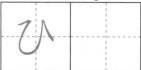

3. ji ka n (time)

4. hi tsu ji (sheep)

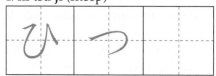

5. chi zu (map)

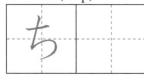

6. su zu shi i (cool – temperature)

7. ka ze (cold – illness; wind)

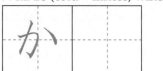

8. ze n ze n (not…at all; never)

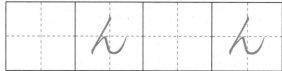

9. **zō** (elephant)

10. **ka zo ku** (family)

The third group of characters written with tenten has two exceptions: "**ji**" and "**zu**." As mentioned, there are two ways to write the sounds "**ji**" and "**zu**," but in most cases they are written with じ and ず. However, ぢ and づ are used in occasional compound words such as "bloody nose" (**ha na ji**) はなぢ and "hammer" (**ka na zu chi**) かなづち.

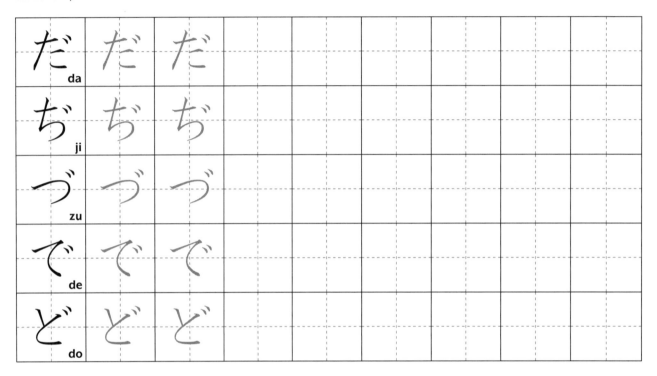

Trace the light grey characters and then complete the word with the correct tenten character.

1. **to mo da chi** (friend)

2. **da re** (who)

3. **de n wa** (telephone)

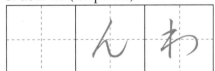

4. **de n ki** (light; electricity)

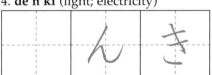

5. **da i do ko ro** (kitchen)

6. **ma do** (window)

The fourth group of characters written with tenten has no exceptions.

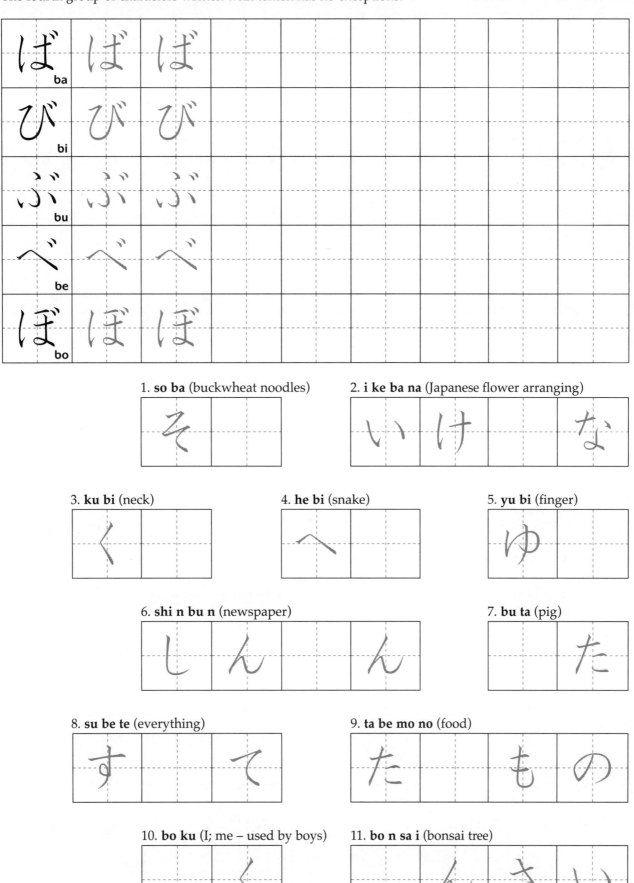

1. **so ba** (buckwheat noodles)

2. **i ke ba na** (Japanese flower arranging)

3. **ku bi** (neck)

4. **he bi** (snake)

5. **yu bi** (finger)

6. **shi n bu n** (newspaper)

7. **bu ta** (pig)

8. **su be te** (everything)

9. **ta be mo no** (food)

10. **bo ku** (I; me – used by boys)

11. **bo n sa i** (bonsai tree)

The small circle or maru (˚) is only added to **"ha,"** **"hi,"** **"fu,"** **"he"** and **"ho."** Trace the light grey characters, and then try writing them in the blank boxes on your own.

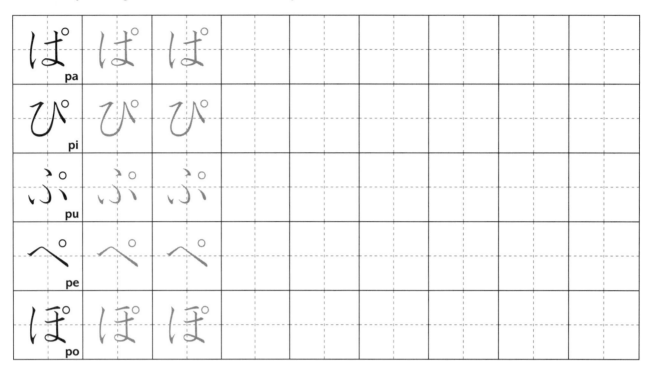

Try writing these words using characters written with maru (˚). Many of these words also use a small **"tsu"** (つ), which is pronounced as a short silent pause. In romaji a small **"tsu"** (つ) is usually indicated by doubling the following consonant (see Rule 3).

1. **su ppa i** (sour)

2. **ra ppa** (trumpet)

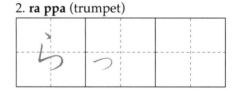

3. **e n pi tsu** (pencil)

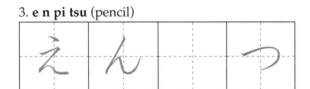

4. **ha ppi** (festival coat)

5. **te n pu ra** (battered, deep-fried food)

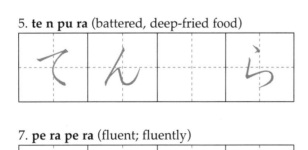

6. **ki ppu** (ticket)

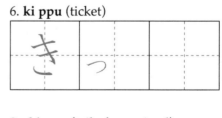

7. **pe ra pe ra** (fluent; fluently)

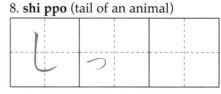

8. **shi ppo** (tail of an animal)

9. **pe ko pe ko** (very hungry)

10. **po ka po ka** (warm feeling)

11. **ri ppa** (splendid; fine)

12. **ha ppa** (leaf)

READING PRACTICE 4: TENTEN AND MARU

You should be able to read the words below now. Fold the page lengthwise (or cover it with your hand) so you can only see the hiragana words on the left half of the page. Try reading them aloud and then check your reading with the rōmaji on the right half of the page. Keep practicing until you can read them all.

ひ ら が な				**hi ra ga na** (hiragana characters)
み ぎ				**mi gi** (right hand side)
い り ぐ ち				**i ri gu chi** (entrance)
げ ん か ん				**ge n ka n** (entryway of a Japanese home)
に ほ ん ご				**ni ho n go** (Japanese)
ひ ざ				**hi za** (knee; lap)
じ か ん				**ji ka n** (time)
ち ず				**chi zu** (map)
か ぜ				**ka ze** (cold – illness; wind)
か ぞ く				**ka zo ku** (family)
だ れ				**da re** (who)
で ん わ				**de n wa** (telephone)
ま ど				**ma do** (window)
い け ば な				**i ke ba na** (flower arranging)
へ び				**he bi** (snake)
し ん ぶ ん				**shi n bu n** (newspaper)
す べ て				**su be te** (all; everything)
ぼ ん さ い				**bo n sa i** (bonsai tree)
ら っ ぱ				**ra ppa** (trumpet)
え ん ぴ つ				**e n pi tsu** (pencil)
き っ ぷ				**ki ppu** (ticket)
ぺ ら ぺ ら				**pe ra pe ra** (fluent; fluently)
し っ ぽ				**shi ppo** (tail of an animal)

RULE 2 COMBINED CHARACTERS

As mentioned in the Introduction there are three special hiragana characters that are used extensively in combination with 11 consonants to form 33 additional sounds (see the chart at the beginning of Section Two). When combined in this way "ya," "yu" and "yo" are written in half-size characters at the bottom left corner, as in the examples below. Many of the example words have a line above the vowel, indicating it is two syllables in length. More information about Japanese long vowels will be explained later (see Rule 4). Trace the light grey characters and then try to complete the example words with the correct combined characters.

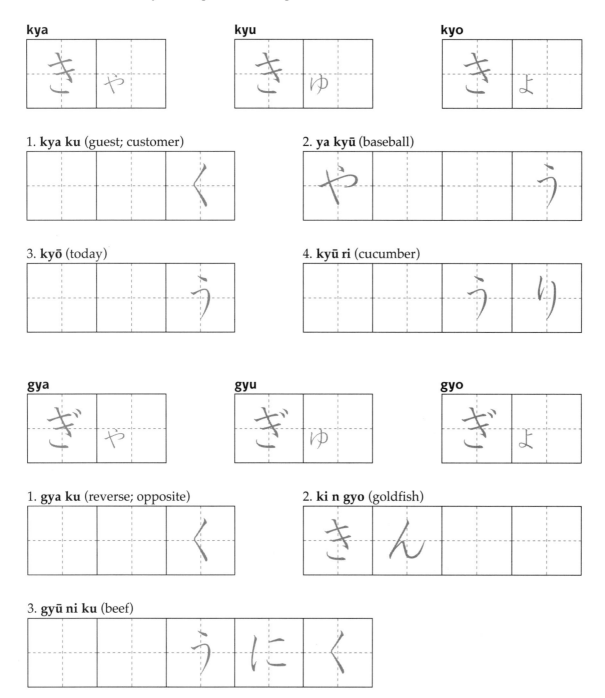

kya

kyu

kyo

1. **kya ku** (guest; customer)

2. **ya kyū** (baseball)

3. **kyō** (today)

4. **kyū ri** (cucumber)

gya

gyu

gyo

1. **gya ku** (reverse; opposite)

2. **ki n gyo** (goldfish)

3. **gyū ni ku** (beef)

sha

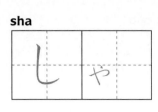

shu

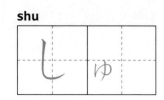

sho

1. **i sha** (medical doctor)

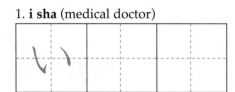

2. **shu fu** (homemaker)

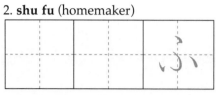

3. **sho ku dō** (dining room; cafeteria)

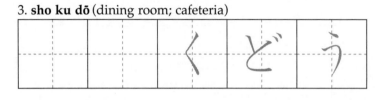

4. **ba sho** (place; location)

ja

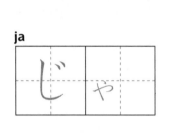

ju

jo

1. **jā ne** (See you later!)

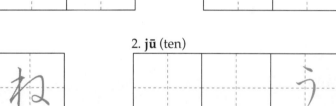

2. **jū** (ten)

3. **ma jo** (witch)

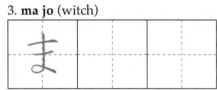

4. **jū sho** (address)

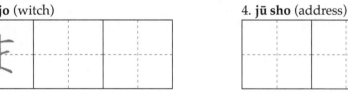

5. **ja ma** (nuisance)

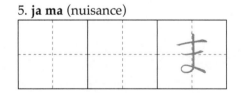

6. **jū dō** (judo)

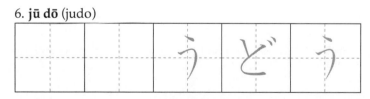

cha

ちゃ

chu

ちゅ

cho

ちょ

1. **o mo cha** (toys)

おも

2. **cho tto** (a little; somewhat)

っと

3. **chū go ku** (China)

うにく

4. **o cha** (green tea)

お

ja

ぢゃ

ju

ぢゅ

jo

ぢょ

The above combined characters are rarely used, and they are usually used for emphasis only.

nya

にゃ

nyu

にゅ

nyo

にょ

1. **gyū nyū** (milk)

ぎゅう　う

2. **nyā** (meow – cry of a cat)

あ

3. **ka nyū** (to subscribe)

か　う

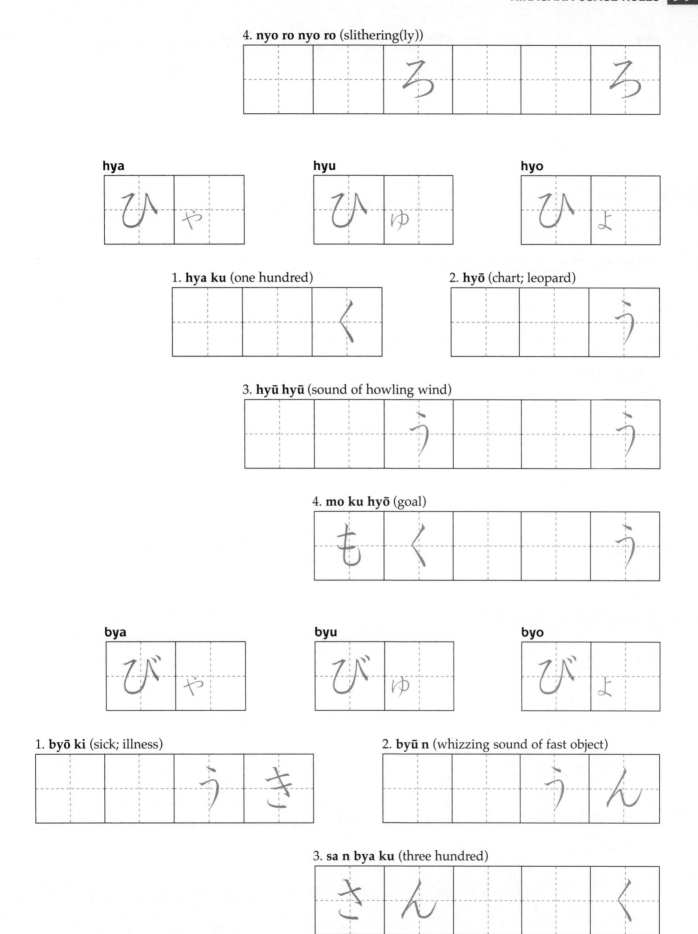

4. **nyo ro nyo ro** (slithering(ly))

hya

hyu

hyo

1. **hya ku** (one hundred)

2. **hyō** (chart; leopard)

3. **hyū hyū** (sound of howling wind)

4. **mo ku hyō** (goal)

bya

byu

byo

1. **byō ki** (sick; illness)

2. **byū n** (whizzing sound of fast object)

3. **sa n bya ku** (three hundred)

pya

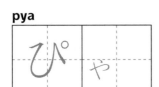

pyu

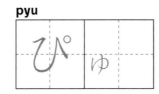

pyo

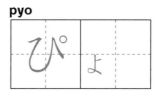

1. **ha ppya ku** (eight hundred)

2. **pyū** (sound of powerful wind)

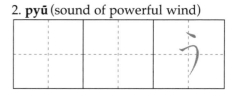

3. **ha ppyō** (announcement; presentation)

4. **ha ppyō ka i** (recital)

mya

myu

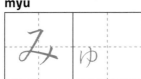

myo

1. **sa n mya ku** (mountain range)

2. **myū** (small pet name)*

3. **ho n myō** (real name)

4. **myō** (strange; unusual)

5. **mya ku** (pulse)

*The character combination "**myu**" is only used in uncommon words not included here.

rya	ryu	ryo
	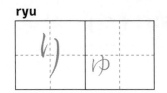	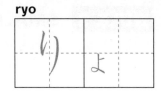

1. **rya ku go** (abbreviation)

2. **ryo kō** (travel)

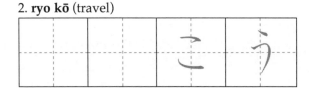

3. **ryū ga ku** (study abroad)

4. **ryō** (dormitory)

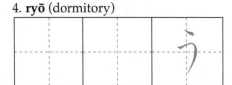

READING PRACTICE 5: COMBINED CHARACTERS

You should be able to read these words with combined characters now. Fold the page lengthwise (or cover it with your hand) so you can only see the words on the left hand side of the page. Try reading them aloud and then check the words on the right. Keep practicing until you can read them all.

き	ゃ	く					**kya ku** (guest; customer)
き	ゅ	う	り				**kyū ri** (cucumber)
き	ょ	う	と				**kyō to** (Kyoto)
き	ん	ぎ	ょ				**ki n gyo** (goldfish)
ぎ	ゅ	う	に	く			**gyū ni ku** (beef)
ぎ	ゃ	く					**gya ku** (opposite; backwards)
い	し	ゃ					**i sha** (doctor)
し	ゅ	ふ					**shu fu** (homemaker)
し	ょ	く	ど	う			**sho ku dō** (dining room; cafeteria)
ま	じ	ょ					**ma jo** (witch)
じ	ゃ	ん	け	ん	ぽ	ん	**jan ken pon** (rock; paper; scissors)
じ	ゅ	う	し	ょ			**jū sho** (address)
お	も	ち	ゃ				**o mo cha** (toys)
ち	ゅ	う	ご	く			**chū go ku** (China)
ち	ょ	う					**chō** (butterfly)
ぎ	ゅ	う	に	ゅ	う		**gyū nyū** (cows' milk)
ひ	ゃ	く					**hya ku** (hundred)
ひ	ょ	う					**hyō** (chart; leopard)
び	ょ	う	き				**byō ki** (sick; sickness)
さ	ん	び	ゃ	く			**sa n bya ku** (three hundred)
み	ょ	う					**myō** (strange; unusual)
り	ょ	う					**ryō** (dormitory)
り	ゅ	う	が	く			**ryū ga ku** (study abroad)

RULE 3 SMALL "TSU" (っ)

As small "**tsu**" (っ) is pronounced as a short silent pause. In rōmaji it is usually indicated by a doubling of the following consonant. One exception is the consonant "**ch**," in which case it is indicated by adding a "**t**" as in "**dotchi**" どっち or "which one; which way." A small "**tsu**" may also be used at the end of a phrase or sentence to indicate a sense of abruptness, anger, or surprise. It is pronounced with a "glottal stop" or in other words, stopping the flow of air by closing back of the throat (epiglottis). Small "**tsu**" is written in the bottom left hand corner, as are small "**ya**," "**yu**," and "**yo**." Complete the example words by tracing the light grey characters and writing a small "**tsu**" in the appropriate area of the blank boxes.

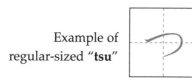

Example of regular-sized "**tsu**"   Example of small "**tsu**"

1. ga kkō (school)

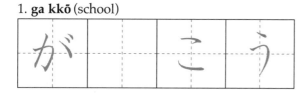

2. a sa tte (day after tomorrow)

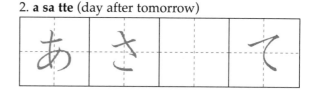

3. ki ssa te n (coffee shop)

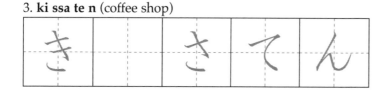

4. ki tte (stamp)

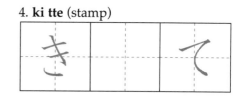

5. ki ppu (ticket)

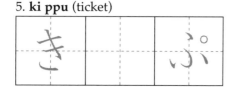

6. ma ssu gu (straight)

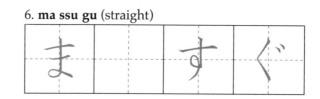

READING PRACTICE 6: SMALL "tsu"

You should be able to read the words below with small "**tsu**" now. Remember to pronounced it as a short silent pause. Check your pronunciation with the phonetic guide on the right. If you don't understand, try reading Rule 3 again.

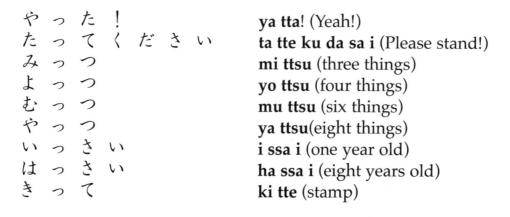

やった！   **ya tta!** (Yeah!)

たってください   **ta tte ku da sa i** (Please stand!)

みっつ   **mi ttsu** (three things)

よっつ   **yo ttsu** (four things)

むっつ   **mu ttsu** (six things)

やっつ   **ya ttsu** (eight things)

いっさい   **i ssa i** (one year old)

はっさい   **ha ssa i** (eight years old)

きって   **ki tte** (stamp)

かった   **ka tta** (I won.)
おもしろかった   **o mo shi ro ka tta** (That was fun.)
いらっしゃいませ   **i ra ssha i ma se** (Welcome! – at stores)
まっすぐ   **ma ssu gu** (straight)
いってください   **i tte ku da sa i** (Please say it.)
にっぽん   **ni ppo n** (Japan – alternative name)

RULE 4   LONG VOWELS

As you have already seen many times, some words in romaji have a line above a vowel, indicating it is a long vowel, or a vowel two syllables in length. Writing most long vowels in hiragana is simple; you add one of the five Japanese vowels あ, い, う, え, お. As already noted, in romaji a long vowel is indicated by a line above the vowel, except "**i**," which is written twice. Read the examples below.

Long "a"	おかあさん	o kā sa n	(mother)
Long "i"	いいえ	i i e	(no)
Long "u"	きゅうり	kyū ri	(cucumber)
Long "e"*	おねえさん	o nē sa n	(older sister)
Long "o"*	おおきい	ō ki i	(big)

* Actually, the last two examples are exceptions. Usually い ("i" as in e**a**sy) makes the long え ("e" as in r**e**d) sound. Take extra care to pronounce an い following a character with the え vowel sound as a long vowel え. At first this may be a bit confusing because in romaji it is usually written with an "I." In this case the romaji reflects the hiragana writing, not the pronunciation.

えいご	e i go (ē go)	(English)
せんせい	se n se i (se n sē)	(teacher)
えいが	e i ga (ē ga)	(movie)
とけい	to ke i (to kē)	(clock)

Likewise, a long vowel お ("o" as in **o**ld) is made by adding う ("u" as in y**ou**th). This book consistently uses a line above the "o" to indicate the long vowel in rōmaji.

さようなら	sa yō n na ra	(goodbye)
ありがとう	a ri ga tō	(thank you)
もういちど	mō i chi do	(one more time)

READING PRACTICE 7: LONG VOWELS

You should be able to read the words below with long vowels now. Cover the right hand side of the page so you can only see the hiragana words. Check your pronunciation with the phonetic guide on the right. If you don't understand, try reading Rule 4 again.

o i shi i (delicious)
o kā sa n (mother)
tō kyō (Tokyo; capital of Japan)
ō ki i (big)
kyū (nine)
ki i ro (yellow)
ki re i (pretty)
hi kō ki (airplane)
o ni i sa n (big brother)
o ha yō (good morning)
o nē sa n (big sister)
ho n shū (Honshū – island of Japan)
o tō sa n (dad)
i i e (no)
kyō (today)
chi i sa i (small)
o tō to (little brother)
yo ne n se i (fourth grader; senior)
jū (ten)
to ke i (clock)
a ri ga tō (Thank you.)
o bā sa n (grandmother)
fū se n (balloon)
jā ne (See you later!)
ga kkō (school)
o ji i sa n (grandfather)

RULE 5 SENTENCE PARTICLES "WA," "E" AND "O"

Japanese uses small grammatical words called "particles" to help the reader understand the relationships between words in a sentence. They are usually one or two hiragana characters in length, and among other things, they indicate the topic, subject, object, location and direction. Particles are always placed directly after the words they mark. Rule 5 simply describes how three hiragana characters are pronounced differently when used as grammatical particles.

"**wa**" The Topic Particle:
When used as a "topic" particle, は is pronounced "**wa**" instead of "**ha**."

Examples: Trace the light grey characters and then write the particle "**wa**" in the blank box. A period in Japanese is written with a small circle in the bottom left corner of its own box. After you have written each sentence, practice reading it and take care to pronounce the particles correctly.

A) I am a (college) student.

watashi	**wa**	**gakusei**	**desu**
(I, me)	(topic)	(student)	(am, are)

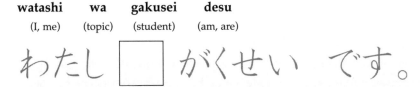
わたし 　□ 　がくせい 　です。

B) What is your telephone number?

o	**denwa bangō**	**wa**	**nan**	**desu**	**ka**
(honorific)	(phone number)	(topic)	(what)	(is, are)	(question particle)

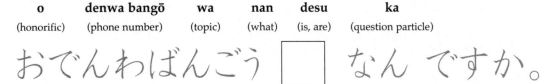
おでんわばんごう 　□ 　なん 　ですか。

"**e**" The Direction Particle:
When used as a "direction" particle, へ is pronounced like え ("**e**" as in r**e**d).

Examples:

A) We are going to Peace Park (Hiroshima).

watashi-tachi	**wa**	**heiwa-kō en**	**e**	**ikimasu**
(we)	(topic)	(Peace Park)	(direction particle)	(will go)

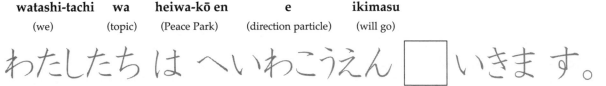
わたしたち は へいわこうえん 　□ 　いきます。

B) Please turn right.

migi	**e**	**magatte**	**kudasai**
(right)	(direction)	(to turn)	(please)

みぎ 　□ 　まがって ください。

"**o**" The Object Particle:
The character を is only used as a particle to mark the "object" of a sentence and it is pronounced like お ("**o**" as in **o**ld).

Examples:

A) I saw Mount Fuji.

watashi	**wa**	**fuji san**	**o**	**mimashit**
(I; me)	(topic)	(Mount Fuji)	(object)	(saw)

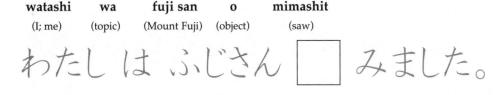
わたし は ふじさん 　□ 　みました。

B) I ate sushi yesterday.

kinō	watashi	wa	sushi	o	tabemashita
(yesterday)	(I; me)	(topic)	(sushi)	(object)	(ate)

きのう わたし は すし ☐ たべました。

READING PRACTICE 8: PARTICLES "wa," "e" AND "o"

You should be able to read some sentences with the particles "wa," "e" and "o" now. Without looking at the phonetic guides on the bottom of the page try reading these sentences. Check your pronunciation when you are done. You may want to repeat this practice to increase accuracy and fluency.

1. せんしゅう は ふゆやすみ でした。

2. わたし は ともだち の うち へ いきました。

3. えいが を みました。

4. ともだち は まいにち おかし を たべます。

5. らいしゅう はいしゃ へ いきます。

6. ともだち は はいしゃ が きらい です。

7. はる やすみ は いつ ですか。

8. どこ へ いきますか。

9. なに を しますか。

10. わたし は らいねん にほん へ りゅうがく します。

11. にほんご を べんきょう します。

1. **sneshū wa fuyu yasumi deshita**   Last week was winter break.
2. **watashi wa tomodachi no uchi e ikimashita**   I went to a friend's house.
3. **eiga o mimashita**   (We) saw a movie.
4. **tomodachi wa mainichi okashi o tabemasu**   My friend eats snacks everyday.
5. **raishū haisha e ikimasu**   (My friend) is going to the dentist next week.
6. **tomodachi wa haisha ga kirai desu**   My friend hates the dentist.
7. **haru yasumi wa itsu desu ka**   When is spring vacation?
8. **doko e ikimasu ka**   Where will you go?
9. **nani o shimasu ka**   What will you do?
10. **watashi wa rainen nihon e ryūgaku shimasu**   I will study abroad in Japan next year.
11. **nihongo o benkyō shimasu**   (I) will study Japanese.

SECTION THREE
Reading and Writing Practice

Commonly Mistaken Hiragana

Commonly Mistaken Combined Characters

Map of Japan

Family Members

Daily Expressions

Numbers

Parts of the Body

Weather

Places at School

In the Classroom

At the Department Store

Japanese Foods

Japanese Lunch Kiosk

Animals

なまえ _____

Commonly Mistaken Hiragana

Part A:
Circle the correct hiragana character.

Part B:
Circle the correct hiragana character.

i	け	こ	り	(い)	き	ま	も		**ko**	ほ	い	に	た	(こ)	も	り
1. **ku**	し	く	つ	て	ん	へ	え		1. **shi**	し	つ	へ	く	ん	て	と
2. **a**	お	ぬ	ゆ	わ	あ	め	ね		2. **o**	や	な	お	め	あ	ね	ぬ
3. **sa**	よ	き	を	ち	せ	け	さ		3. **ki**	さ	よ	を	ち	ま	も	き
4. **ta**	た	な	さ	は	も	こ	い		4. **na**	た	な	き	は	ほ	も	よ
5. **nu**	あ	め	わ	ぬ	お	な	ま		5. **me**	ぬ	お	あ	ゆ	わ	め	ね
6. **ne**	れ	ね	わ	あ	お	ゆ	の		6. **re**	ぬ	そ	わ	ね	れ	あ	つ
7. **wa**	ね	あ	れ	め	ぬ	わ	つ		7. **ro**	ろ	そ	る	を	よ	と	え
8. **ma**	も	き	ま	に	こ	た	ほ		8. **ho**	は	ま	き	ほ	さ	こ	た
9. **su**	む	る	ぬ	す	み	ね	ま		9. **mu**	す	む	み	ま	ね	ぬ	る
10. **ri**	い	り	こ	ら	う	そ	え		10. **ru**	ろ	そ	と	よ	む	す	る
11. **ra**	う	え	む	ら	お	や	な		11. **u**	ら	え	や	う	お	む	な
12. **ke**	い	に	り	ほ	は	せ	け		12. **se**	は	け	に	た	は	せ	り
13. **so**	ろ	と	て	こ	え	そ	ん		13. **chi**	さ	つ	た	ろ	ち	を	そ
14. **tsu**	て	う	ら	つ	め	わ	ち		14. **te**	そ	く	て	し	つ	へ	ん
15. **ni**	こ	い	り	た	に	ほ	は		15. **no**	の	て	あ	ぬ	め	つ	う
16. **ha**	ほ	け	は	に	な	も	ま		16. **mo**	ま	き	も	ほ	け	は	し
17. **ya**	か	な	つ	う	や	ら	め		17. **e**	ん	き	う	ら	れ	え	そ

Time _____:_____

Time _____:_____

なまえ _____

Commonly Mistaken Combined Characters

Part A:
Circle the correct combined character.

Part B:
Circle the correct combined character.

	gyo	きょ	じょ	(ぎょ)	びょ		**kyo**	びょ	ぎょ	きゅ	(きょ)
1.	**shu**	しゃ	しゅ	じゅ	ちゅ	1.	**ju**	しゅ	じゅ	じゃ	じょ
2.	**cho**	ちゃ	ぢゃ	しょ	ちょ	2.	**nyo**	にょ	にゅ	りゅ	ちゅ
3.	**myu**	みゅ	みょ	みゃ	ちゅ	3.	**nyu**	にゅ	にゃ	にょ	りゅ
4.	**bya**	ぴゃ	ひゃ	びゃ	びょ	4.	**hya**	ひゅ	みゅ	りゅ	ひゃ
5.	**gyu**	ぎゃ	きゅ	きょ	ぎゅ	5.	**myo**	みゃ	りょ	みょ	ちょ
6.	**nya**	にゅ	にゃ	りゃ	にょ	6.	**byu**	びゅ	ぴゅ	ひゅ	きゅ
7.	**rya**	りゃ	にょ	りゅ	りょ	7.	**ryo**	りゃ	りょ	ぴょ	りゅ
8.	**pyu**	ぴゃ	ひゅ	ぴょ	ぴゅ	8.	**hyu**	ぴゅ	ひゃ	びゅ	ひゅ
9.	**jo**	じゃ	しょ	じょ	じゅ	9.	**chu**	ちゃ	しゅ	ちゅ	しゃ
10.	**kya**	ぎゃ	きゅ	きょ	きゃ	10.	**ja**	しゃ	じゃ	しゅ	じゅ
11.	**hyo**	ひゅ	ひょ	ぴょ	びょ	11.	**cha**	しゃ	ちゅ	ちゃ	ちょ
12.	**pyo**	ひょ	ぴょ	びょ	ぴゅ	12.	**ryu**	りゅ	りゃ	ちゃ	りょ
13.	**kyu**	きゃ	ぎゅ	きゅ	きょ	13.	**gya**	ぎゃ	しゅ	しゃ	ぎゅ
14.	**sho**	しゅ	じゅ	しょ	じょ	14.	**sha**	しゅ	しゃ	じゃ	じゅ
15.	**byo**	ひょ	びゅ	ぴょ	びょ	15.	**pya**	ぴゅ	びゃ	ぴゃ	ひゃ

Time _____:_____

Time _____:_____

Map of Japan

なまえ _____

Japan (**ni ho n**)

Major Islands of Japan

1. Hokkaido (**ho kka i dō**)

2. Honshu (**ho n shū**)

3. Shikoku (**shi ko ku**)

4. Kyushu (**kyū shū**)

5. Okinawa (**o ki na wa**)

North (**ki ta**)

Major Cities

6. Sapporo (**sa ppo ro**)

7. Aomori (**a o mo ri**)

8. Sendai (**se n da i**)

9. Nagano (**na ga no**)

10. Tokyo – capital (**tō kyō**)

11. Yokohama (**yo ko ha ma**)

12. Nagoya (**na go ya**)

13. Kobe (**kō be**)

14. Kyoto (**kyō to**)

15. Osaka (**ō sa ka**)

16. Hiroshima (**hi ro shi ma**)

17. Fukuoka (**fu ku o ka**)

なまえ _____

Family Members

と	も	わ	お	か	あ	さ	ん	お	え	お
お	う	た	か	ね	い	お	じ	さ	ん	と
に	と	し	へ	つ	し	ひ	す	た	あ	う
い	く	い	も	う	と	さ	て	ぼ	こ	さ
さ	せ	お	よ	み	お	ほ	ん	く	な	ん
ん	ち	ば	の	り	ば	ね	ら	か	め	お
あ	か	さ	ふ	を	あ	や	え	ゆ	ま	と
じ	ぬ	ん	む	れ	さ	い	と	さ	ん	う
し	お	じ	い	さ	ん	け	そ	き	ん	と

1. I; myself – only boys (**bo ku**)

2. grandfather (**o ji i sa n**)

3. I; myself (**wa ta shi**)

4. grandmother (**o bā sa n**)

5. younger sister (**i mō to**)

6. father (**o tō sa n**)

7. younger brother (**o tō to**)

8. mother (**o kā sa n**)

9. uncle (**o ji sa n**)

10. older brother (**o ni i sa n**)

11. aunt (**o ba sa n**)

12. older sister (**o nē sa n**)

なまえ _____

Daily Expressions

You're welcome! (**dō i ta shi mas hi te**)
Sounds like "Don't touch my mustache!"

DOWN

1. Excuse me. (**su mi ma se n**)
2. Hello!; Good afternoon! (**ko n ni chi wa***)
4. How are you? (**o ge n ki de su ka**)
5. Good night! (**o ya su mi na sa i**)
6. I'm sorry. (**go me n na sa i**)
10. You're welcome! (**dō i ta shi ma shi te**)
11. No. (**i i e**)

ACROSS

3. Good evening! (**ko n ba n wa***)
4. Good morning! (**o ha yō go za i ma su**)
7. I'm fine. (**ge n ki de su**)
8. Goodbye! (**sa yō na ra**)
9. Thank you. (**a ri ga tō go za i ma su**)
12. Yes. (**ha i**)

なまえ _____

Numbers

Read the numbers in hiragana and connect them in the chart below. What do you see in the picture?

Start: きゅう(9)→	じゅうはち(18)→	にじゅうなな→	さんじゅうなな→	よんじゅうろく↓
↓ ななじゅうさん	←ろくじゅうさん	←ろくじゅうよん	←ごじゅうご	←ごじゅうろく
ななじゅうに→	はちじゅういち→	きゅうじゅういち→	きゅうじゅうに→	はちじゅうさん ↓
↓ きゅうじゅうよん	←はちじゅうよん	←ななじゅうご	←ななじゅうよん	←ななじゅうさん
はちじゅうご→	ななじゅうご→	ななじゅうろく→	ろくじゅうなな→	ごじゅうなな ↓
↓ さんじゅう	←さんじゅうきゅう	←にじゅうはち	←さんじゅうなな	←よんじゅうなな
にじゅう→	きゅう	Finished!		

1	2	3	4	5	6	7	8	9	10
11	12	13	14	15	16	17	18	19	20
21	22	23	24	25	26	27	28	29	30
31	32	33	34	35	36	37	38	39	40
41	42	43	44	45	46	47	48	49	50
51	52	53	54	55	56	57	58	59	60
61	62	63	64	65	66	67	68	69	70
71	72	73	74	75	76	77	78	79	80
81	82	83	84	85	86	87	88	89	90
91	92	93	94	95	96	97	98	99	100

(Hint: see page 82)

Counting in Japanese

1	いち	11	じゅういち	30	さんじゅう
2	に	12	じゅうに	40	よんじゅう；しじゅう
3	さん	13	じゅうさん	50	ごじゅう
4	よん；し	14	じゅうよん；じゅうし	60	ろくじゅう
5	ご	15	じゅうご	70	ななじゅう；しちじゅう
6	ろく	16	じゅうろく	80	はちじゅう
7	なな；しち	17	じゅうなな；じゅうしち	90	きゅうじゅう
8	はち	18	じゅうはち	100	ひゃく
9	きゅう；く	19	じゅうきゅう；じゅうく		
10	じゅう	20	にじゅう		

なまえ _____

Parts of the Body

1. head (**a ta ma**)

2. shoulders (**ka ta**)

3. knees (**ni za**)

4. legs; feet (**a shi**)

5. hands (**te**)

6. eyes (**me**)

7. ears (**mi mi**)

8. mouth (**ku chi**)

9. nose (**ha na**)

10. hair (**ka mi**)

11. stomach (**o na ka**)

12. back (**se na ka**)

13. face (**ka o**)

14. teeth (**ha**)

15. throat (**no do**)

16. neck (**ku bi**)

17. wrist (**te ku bi**)

18. ankle (**a shi ku bi**)

19. chest (**mu ne**)

20. arm (**u de**)

21. finger (**yu bi**)

22. fingernail (**tsu me**)

23. elbow (**hi ji**)

24. body (**ka ra da**)

Common Expressions with Body Vocabulary

smart	あたま が いい	(literally "head is good")
dumb; unintelligent	あたま が わるい	(literally "head is bad")
poor hearing; deaf	みみ が とおい	(literally "ears are far")
bad eyesight	め が わるい	(literally "eyes are bad")
hungry	おなか が すいた	(literally "stomach became empty")
thirsty	のど が かわいた	(literally "throat became dry")

なまえ _____

Weather

1. weather (**te n ki**)

2. clear; fine (**ha re**)

3. rain (**a me**)

4. cloudy (**ku mo ri**)

5. snow (**yu ki**)

6. storm (**a ra shi**)

7. windy (**ka ze ga tsu yo i**)

8. hot (**a tsu i**)

9. cold (**sa mu i**)

Describe today's weather as in the example below.

Today's weather is <u>clear</u>.	きょう	の	てんき	は	はれ	です。
	Today	's	weather	"topic" particle	fine	is; am; are

Try recording the weather for a month. Use hiragana to write the appropriate weather word(s) on the calendar below. Each time you record the weather, try describing it in Japanese.

にち Sunday	げつ Monday	か Tuesday	すい Wednesday	もく Thursday	きん Friday	ど Saturday
(date)	(date)	(date)	(date)	(date)	(date)	(date)
(date)	(date)	(date)	(date)	(date)	(date)	(date)
(date)	(date)	(date)	(date)	(date)	(date)	(date)
(date)	(date)	(date)	(date)	(date)	(date)	(date)
(date)	(date)	(date)	(date)	(date)	(date)	(date)

なまえ _____

Places at School

1. kindergarten (yō chi e n)	2. elementary school (shō ga kkō)	3. junior high school (chū ga kkō)	4. high school (kō kō)
幼	小	中	高
5. college; university (da i ga ku)	6. classroom (kyō shi tsu)	7. health center (ho ke n shi tsu)	8. library (to sho shi tsu)
大	E–Mc²		
9. music room (o n ga ku shi tsu)	10. cafeteria* (sho ku dō)	11. athletic field (u n dō jō)	12. gym (ta i i ku ka n)

13. To which places do students usually bring books (please circle any that apply)?

きょうしつ　　　　ほけんしつ　　　　としょしつ　　　　たいいくかん

14. Which schools come after Jr. High School (please circle any that apply)?

だいがく　　　　しょうがっこう　　　　こうこう　　　　ようちえん

15. Which places are usually found indoors (please circle any that apply)?

としょしつ　　　　ほけんしつ　　　　うんどうじょう　　　　おんがくしつ

*Japanese students (except university students) generally eat lunch in the classroom.

なまえ _____

In the Classroom

1. pencil (e n pi tsu)	2. paper (ka mi)	3. scissors (ha sa mi)	4. book (ho n)
5. glue (no ri)	6. chair (i su)	7. desk (tsu ku e)	8. ruler (jō gi)
9. calculator (de n ta ku)	10. window (ma do)	11. light (de n ki)	12. clock (to ke i)

13. Which objects could you fit into a backpack (circle any that apply)?

　　かみ　　　　のり　　　　いす　　　　ほん　　　　えんぴつ　　　　つくえ

14. Which objects are too big to fit into a desk (circle any that apply)?

　　いす　　　はさみ　　　まど　　　じょうぎ　　　のり　　　　でんき

15. Which objects require electricity/batteries (circle any that apply)?

　　とけい　　　　まど　　　　でんたく　　　えんぴつ　　　でんき　　　　のり

なまえ _____

At the Department Store

Write in English and Japanese the appropriate floor of each item.

Example: clocks   <u>8th floor</u>

は	ち	か	い

1. kimono (**ki mo no**) _____

2. toys (**o mo cha**) _____

3. hats (**bō shi**) _____

4. books (**ho n**) _____

5. groceries (**sho ku hi n**) _____

6. rings (**yu bi wa**) _____

7. bags (**ka ba n**) _____

8. shoes (**ku tsu**) _____

9. suits (**se bi ro**) _____

10. gloves (**te bu ku ro**) _____

おもちゃ	10th floor (**ju kka i** or **ji kkai**)
ほん	9th floor (**kyū ka i**)
とけい	8th floor (**ha chi ka i**)
かばん	7th floor (**na na ka i**)
きもの	6th floor (**ro kka i**)
せびろ	5th floor (**go ka i**)
ぼうし	4th floor (**yo n ka i**)
てぶくろ	3th floor (**sa n ga i**)
くつ	2nd floor (**ni ka i**)
ゆびわ	1st floor (**i kka i**)
しょくひん	Basement 1st floor (**chi ka ikka i**)

なまえ _____

Japanese Foods

1. rice (**go ha n**)	2. riceballs (**o ni gi ri**)	2. box lunch (**o be n tō**)
4. sushi (**su shi**)	5. sliced raw fish (**sa shi mi**)	6. thick white noodles (**u do n**)
7. buckwheat noodles (**so ba**)	8. chilled soba (**za ru so ba**)	9. fried noodles (**ya ki so ba**)
10. roasted chicken and vegetable kabob (**ya ki to ri**)	11. battered and deep-fried seafood and vegetables (**te n pu ra**)	12. roasted sweet potato (**ya ki i mo**)

なまえ _____

Japanese Lunch Kiosk

Read the menu and answer the questions below.

おにぎり	130 えん	やきいも	300 えん
ごはん	200 えん	やきとり	400 えん
うどん	350 えん	ぎゅうにゅう	200 えん
そば	350 えん	おちゃ	200 えん
やきそば	400 えん	こうちゃ	200 えん
ざるそば	350 えん	みず	0 えん
すし　べんとう	500 えん		
てりやき　べんとう	650 えん		
てんぷら　べんとう	750 えん		

Tell the price of the following lunch menu items.

Example: tempera box lunch (**te n pu ra be n tō**)? <u>750 えん</u>

1. How much is the sushi box lunch (**su shi be n tō**)? _____

2. How much is a rice ball (**o ni gi ri**)? _____

3. How much are the soba – buckwheat noodles (**so ba**)? _____

4. How much are the yakitori – roasted chicken and vegetables on a stick (**ya ki to ri**)? _____

5. How much is rice (**go ha n**)? _____

6. What would you pay for green tea (**o cha**) and yakisoba – fried noodles (**ya ki so ba**)? _____

7. What would you pay for water (**mi zu**) and a tempura box lunch (**te ri ya ki be n tō**)? _____

8. What would you pay for milk (**gyū nyū**) and chilled soba noodles (**za ru so ba**)? _____

なまえ _____

Animals

Animals are generally found in one of three environments: 1. as a pet, 2. in the wild or zoo, or 3. on a farm.
Write the name of each animal in hiragana in an appropriate category below.

☐ Snake (**he bi**)   ☐ Bear (**ku ma**)
☐ Dog (**i nu**)   ☐ Pig (**bu ta**)
☐ Cow (**u shi**)   ☐ Elephant (**zō**)
☐ Bird (**to ri**)   ☐ Horse (**u ma**)
☐ Giraffe (**ki ri n**)   ☐ Goldfish (**ki n gyo**)
☐ Rabbit (**u sa gi**)   ☐ Cat (**ne ko**)
☐ Chicken (**ni wa to ri**)   ☐ Fox (**ki tsu ne**)
☐ Monkey (**sa ru**)   ☐ Alligator (**wa ni**)
☐ Turtle (**ka me**)   ☐ Deer (**shi ka**)
☐ Tiger (**to ra**)   ☐ Frog (**ka e ru**)
☐ Sheep (**hi tsu ji**)   ☐ Squirrel (**ri su**)

Pets	Wild/Zoo	Farm

Answers

Commonly Mistaken Hiragana (page 80) Part A 1. く 2. あ 3. さ 4. た 5. ぬ 6. ね 7. わ 8. ま 9. す 10. り 11. ら 12. け 13. そ 14. つ 15. に 16. は 17. や **Part B** 1. し 2. お 3. き 4. な 5. め 6. れ 7. ろ 8. ほ 9. む 10. る 11. う 12. せ 13. ち 14. て 15. の 16. も 17. え

Commonly Mistaken Combined Characters (page 81) Part A 1. しゅ 2. ちょ 3. みゅ 4. びゃ 5. ぎゅ 6. にゃ 7. りゃ 8. ぴゅ 9. じょ 10. きゃ 11. ひょ 12. ぴょ 13. きゅ 14. しょ 15. びょ **Part B** 1. じゅ 2. にょ 3. にゅ 4. ぴゃ 5. みょ 6. びゅ 7. りょ 8. ひゅ 9. ちゅ 10. じゃ 11. ちゃ 12. りゅ 13. ぎゃ 14. しゃ 15. ぴゃ

Map of Japan (page 82) にほん (Japan), きた (North) 1. ほっかいどう 2. ほんしゅう 3. しこく 4. きゅうしゅう 5. おきなわ 6. さっぽろ 7. あおもり 8. せんだい 9. ながの 10. とうきょう 11. よこはま 12. なごや 13. こうべ 14. きょうと 15. おおさか 16. ひろしま 17. ふくおか

Family Members (page 83) 1. おじいさん 2. おばあさん 3. おとうさん 4. おかあさん 5. おにいさん 6. ぼく 7. おとうと 8. いもうと 9. おじさん 10. おばさん 11. わたし 12. おねえさん

Daily Expressions (page 84) <u>DOWN</u> 1. すみません 2. こんにちは 4. おげんきですか 5. おやすみなさい 6. ごめんなさい 10. どういたしまして 11. いいえ <u>ACROSS</u> 3. こんばんは 4. おはようございます 7. げんきです 8. さようなら 9. ありがとうございます 12. はい

Numbers (page 85) 9→18→27→37→46→56→55→64→63→73→72→81→91→92→83→73→74→75→84→94→85→75→76→67→57→47→37→28→39→30→20→9 Finished! (Pictured: Map of Japan)

Parts of the Body (page 86) 1. あたま 2. かた 3. ひざ 4. あし 5. て 6. め 7. みみ 8. くち 9. はな 10. かみ 11. おなか 12. せなか 13. かお 14. は 15. のど 16. くび 17. てくび 18. あしくび 19. むね 20. うで 21. ゆび 22. つめ 23. ひじ 24. からだ

Weather (page 87) 1. てんき 2. はれ 3. あめ 4. くもり 5. ゆき 6. あらし 7. かぜがつよい 8. あつい 9. さむい

Places at School (page 88) 1. ようちえん 2. しょうがっこう 3. ちゅうがっこう 4. こうこう 5. だいがく 6. きょうしつ 7. ほけんしつ 8. としょしつ 9. おんがくしつ 10. しょくどう 11. うんどうじょう 12. たいいくかん 13. きょうしつ、としょしつ 14. だいがく、こうこう 15. としょしつ、ほけんしつ、おんがくしつ

In the Classroom (page 89) 1. えんぴつ 2. かみ 3. はさみ 4. ほん 5. のり 6. いす 7. つくえ 8. じょうぎ 9. でんたく 10. まど 11. でんき 12. とけい 13. かみ、のり、ほん、えんぴつ 14. いす、まど、でんき 15. とけい、でんたく、でんき

At the Department Store (page 90) 1. (6th) ろっかい 2. (10th) じゅっかい or じっかい 3. (4th) よんかい 4. (9th) きゅうかい 5. (B1) ちかいっかい 6. (1st) いっかい 7. (7th) ななかい 8. (2nd) にかい 9. (5th) ごかい 10. (3rd) さんがい

Japanese Foods (page 91) 1. ごはん 2. おにぎり 3. おべんとう 4. すし 5. さしみ 6. うどん 7. そば 8. ざるそば 9. やきそば 10. やきとり 11. てんぷら 12. やきいも

Japanese Lunch Kiosk (page 92) 1. 500えん 2. 130えん 3. 350えん 4. 400えん 5. 200えん 6. 600えん 7. 650えん 8. 550えん

Animals (page 93) **Pets** (いぬ、とり、かめ、きんぎょ、ねこ、かえる) **Zoo** (へび、きりん、さる、とら、くま、ぞう、きつね、わに、しか、りす) **Farm** (うし、うさぎ、にわとり、ひつじ、ぶた、うま)

FLASH CARDS

Suggested Activities

As mentioned in the Introduction it is much easier to learn to read hiragana than to write it. With the right kinds of activities, diligent students can learn to read the basic 46 hiragana in a few hours. You will more readily learn the writing once you have mastered hiragana reading recognition, so it is suggested you begin with the flash cards at the end of the book.

Separate the flash cards by tearing or cutting along the perforated lines. If you are unfamiliar with hiragana take the time to read the front and back of each flash card, paying close attention to the number and type of strokes used in each character. Many hiragana characters look similar, and it is the number and type of strokes that will help to tell them apart.

Hiragana Flash Card Drills (alone or with a partner): It is helpful to start with a few, perhaps 10 flash cards. You can test your reading recognition skills using the "smiley face" and "frowny face" diagrams below. Shuffle the flash cards and look at them one at a time. Say the name of the hiragana character on the top flash card, then look at the back to see if you got it right. If so, place it on the "smiley face." If not, place it on the "frowny face." Continue looking at the flash cards one at a time, and placing them in the appropriate pile. When you are finished, you will know which hiragana characters you can read and which ones need more practice. Now put aside the ones you already know and study the flash cards you had difficulty with. When ready, repeat the activity with the difficult ones. As you gain mastery add more flash cards, until you know all 46! You can repeat this simple activity from time to time to refresh your basic hiragana reading skills.

Hiragana Chart Activity (alone or with a small group): This is an excellent activity to improve your hiragana recognition skills and become familiar with **gojūon** order—the way dictionaries, web searches, etc, are organized. Place all the flash cards on a large surface (i.e. the floor) face up, in random order. Then, try to put them into order as quickly as possible. For an extra challenge use a stopwatch.

Hiragana Pick-up (small group): Place all the flash cards on a large surface face up, in order or mixed up. One person calls the name of a hiragana character and the other players try to quickly put their hand on it. The first one gets to keep it. Continue playing and when all the flash cards are gone, count to see who has the most. The winner gets to be the "caller" for the next game!

Acknowledgements

I am deeply grateful to the many individuals who have contributed valuable comments and suggestions on this book. I am particularly grateful to former colleagues at the American School in Japan: Clark Tenney, Keiko Yasuno, Keiko Ando, Sumino Hirano, Mariko Smisson, Jo Ash, Anita Gesling, Maki Ushigome, Machiko Romaine, Naoko Pennell, and Leslie Birkland. Many others offered their support, and I wish to sincerely thank Dr. Masakazu Watabe, LaNae Stout, Linda Gerber, Shauna Stout, and Ricky Stout. I also wish to thank the helpful people at Tuttle Publishing.

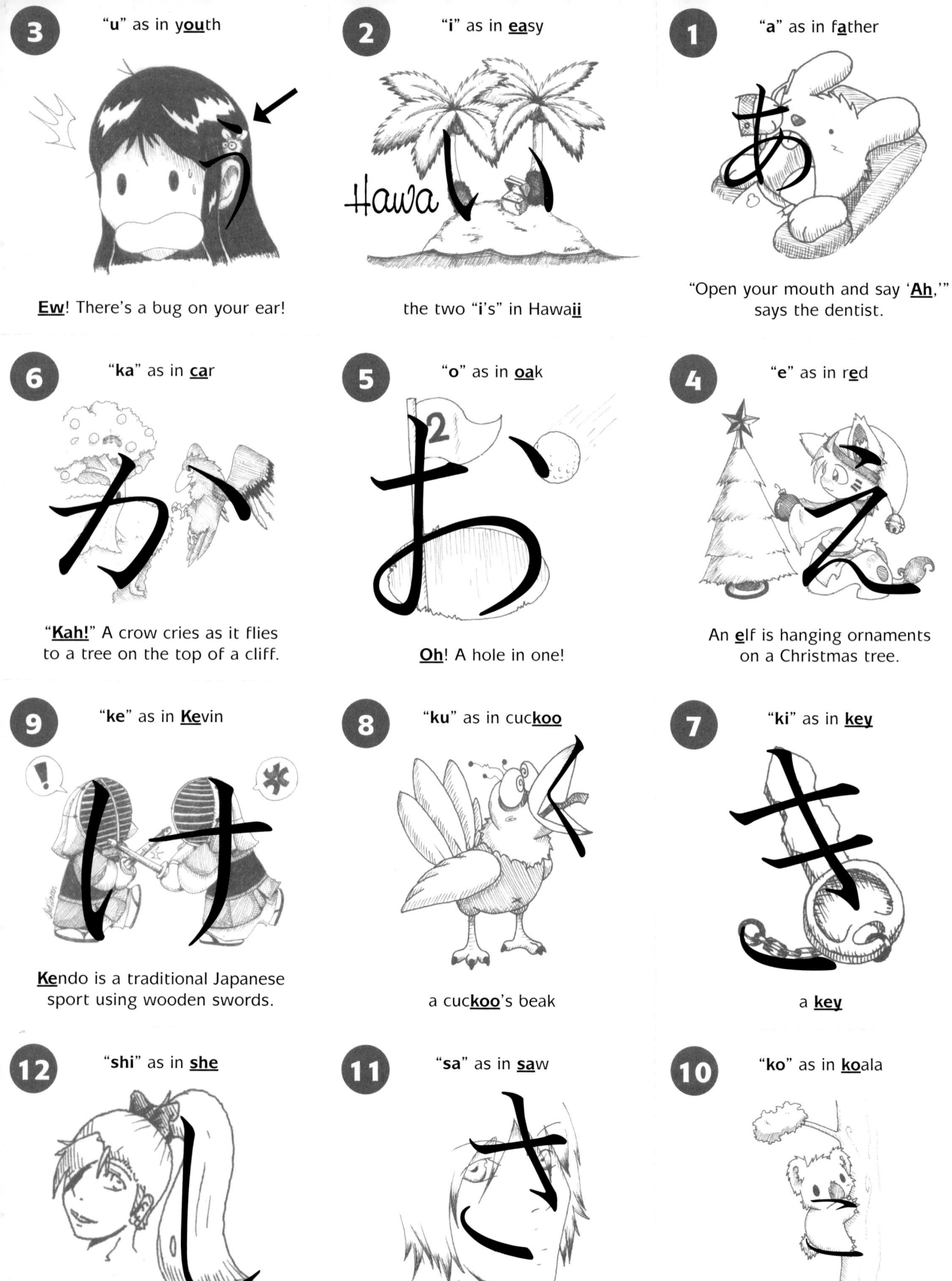

3 "u" as in y**ou**th

Ew! There's a bug on your ear!

2 "i" as in **ea**sy

the two "i's" in Hawa**ii**

1 "a" as in f**a**ther

"Open your mouth and say '**Ah**,'" says the dentist.

6 "ka" as in **ca**r

"**Kah!**" A crow cries as it flies to a tree on the top of a cliff.

5 "o" as in **oa**k

Oh! A hole in one!

4 "e" as in r**e**d

An **e**lf is hanging ornaments on a Christmas tree.

9 "ke" as in **Ke**vin

Kendo is a traditional Japanese sport using wooden swords.

8 "ku" as in cuc**koo**

a cuc**koo**'s beak

7 "ki" as in **ke**y

a **ke**y

12 "shi" as in **she**

She has a ponytail.

11 "sa" as in **sa**w

He **sa**w something that made him smile.

10 "ko" as in **ko**ala

A **ko**ala is climbing a tree.

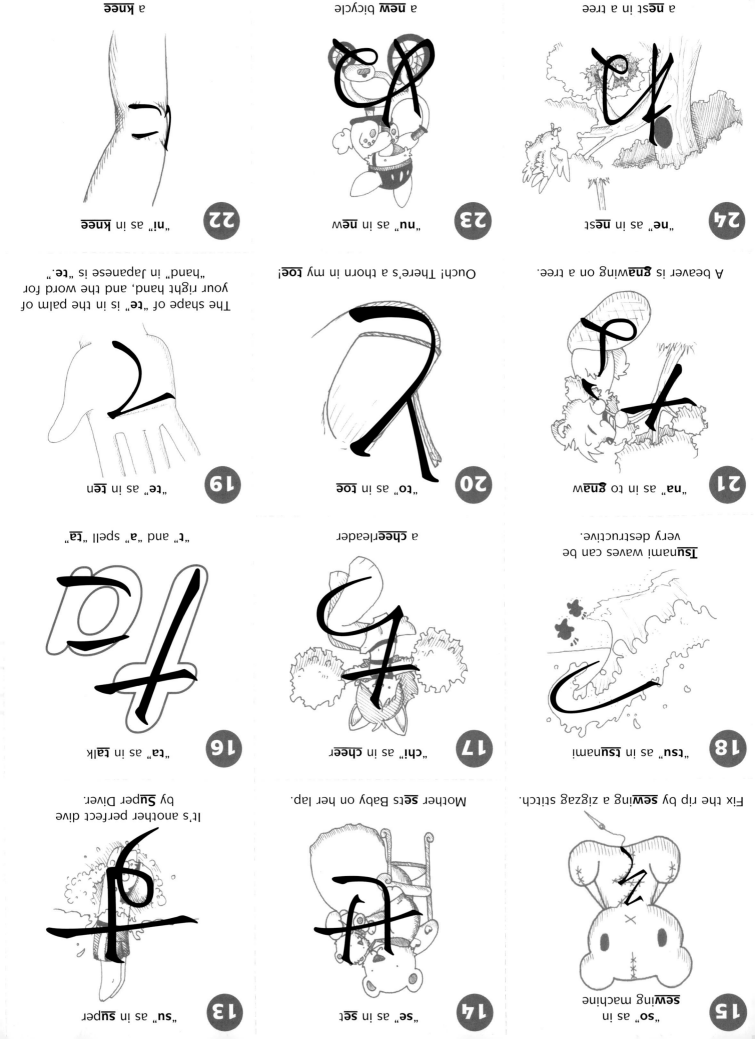

22 "ni" as in knee — a knee

23 "nu" as in new — a new bicycle

24 "ne" as in nest — a nest in a tree

19 "te" as in ten — The shape of "te" is in the palm of your right hand, and the word for "hand" in Japanese is "te."

20 "to" as in toe — Ouch! There's a thorn in my toe!

21 "na" as in to gnaw — A beaver is gnawing on a tree.

16 "ta" as in talk — "t" and "a" spell "ta."

17 "chi" as in cheer — a cheerleader

18 "tsu" as in tsunami — Tsunami waves can be very destructive.

13 "su" as in super — It's another perfect dive by Super Diver.

14 "se" as in set — Mother sets Baby on her lap.

15 "so" as in sewing machine — Fix the rip by sewing a zigzag stitch.

の	は	ひ
ふ	へ	ほ
ま	み	む
め	も	や

27 "hi" as in he

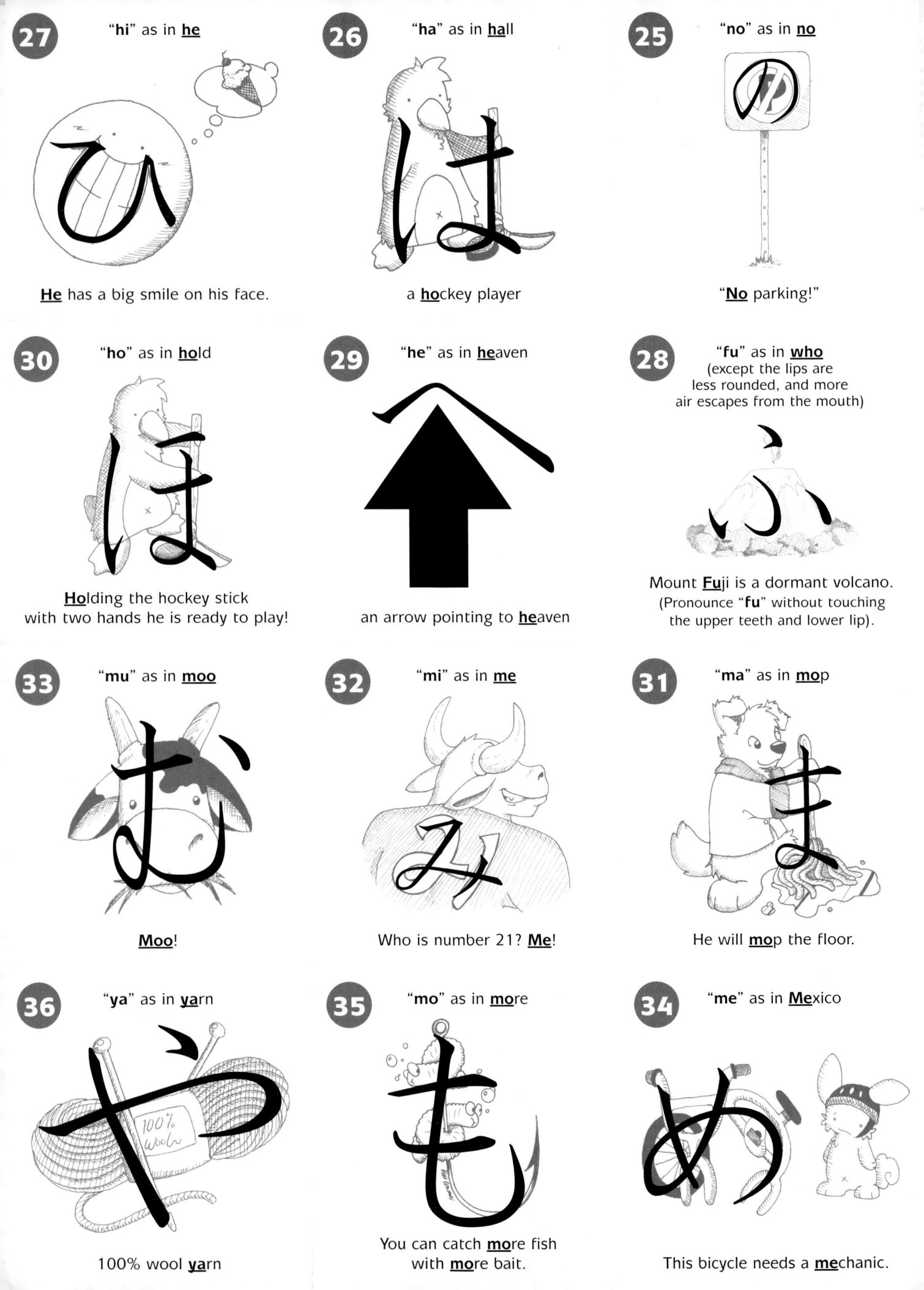

He has a big smile on his face.

26 "ha" as in hall

a hockey player

25 "no" as in no

"No parking!"

30 "ho" as in hold

Holding the hockey stick
with two hands he is ready to play!

29 "he" as in heaven

an arrow pointing to heaven

28 "fu" as in who
(except the lips are
less rounded, and more
air escapes from the mouth)

Mount Fuji is a dormant volcano.
(Pronounce "fu" without touching
the upper teeth and lower lip).

33 "mu" as in moo

Moo!

32 "mi" as in me

Who is number 21? Me!

31 "ma" as in mop

He will mop the floor.

36 "ya" as in yarn

100% wool yarn

35 "mo" as in more

You can catch more fish
with more bait.

34 "me" as in Mexico

This bicycle needs a mechanic.

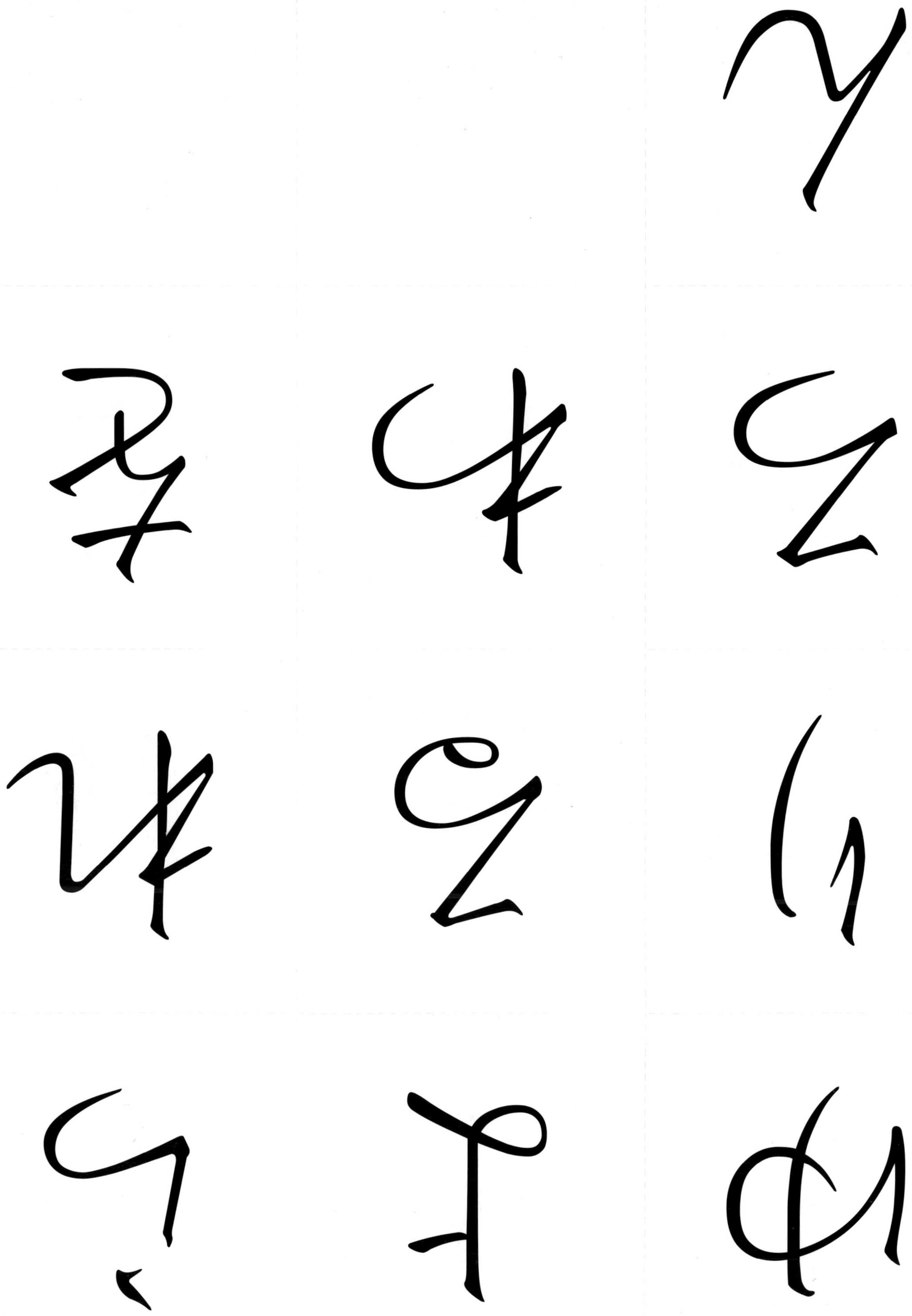

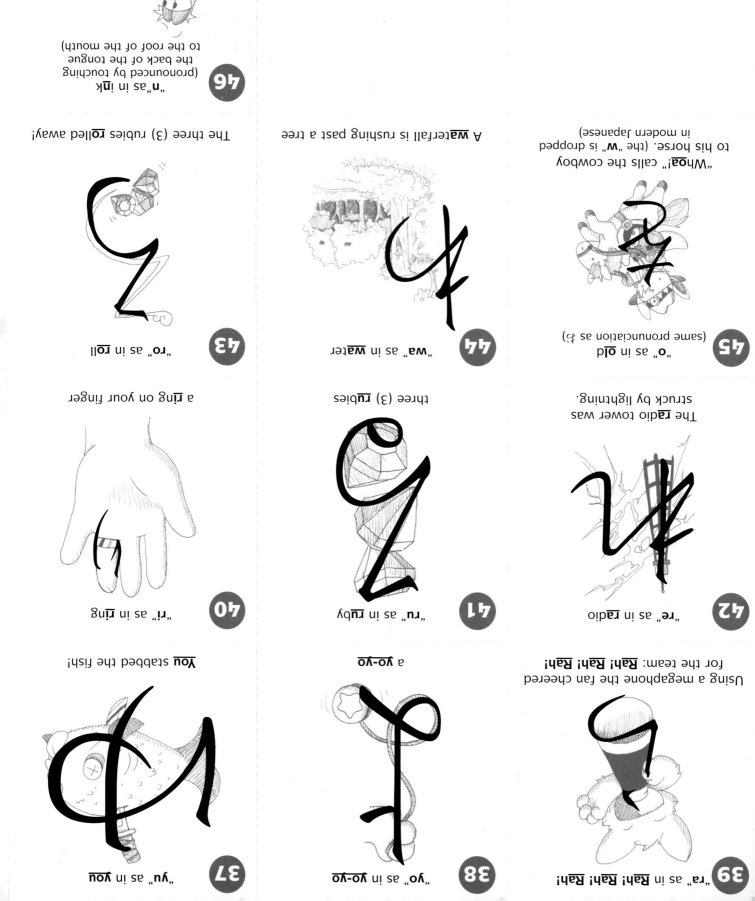

46 "n" as in ink (pronounced by touching the back of the tongue to the roof of the mouth)

The single consonant syllable "n" looks and sounds a little like the English letter "n."

43 "ro" as in roll

The three (3) rubies rolled away!

44 "wa" as in water

A waterfall is rushing past a tree

45 "o" as in old (same pronunciation as を)

"Whoa!" calls the cowboy to his horse. (the "w" is dropped in modern Japanese)

40 "ri" as in ring

a ring on your finger

41 "ru" as in ruby

three (3) rubies

42 "re" as in radio

The radio tower was struck by lightning.

37 "yu" as in you

You stabbed the fish!

38 "yo" as in yo-yo

a yo-yo

39 "ra" as in Rah! Rah! Rah!

Using a megaphone the fan cheered for the team: Rah! Rah! Rah!